When s̶h̶I.T. Happens 2 you...

One Man and his dog's mission to rid the world of I.T. Woes, Worries & Peculiarities that affect your business...

By Chris Blunt

Entrepreneur, IT Guru and Head of Making things work at one of the UKs most loved I.T. Companies...

Copyright

When shI.T. Happens 2 you: One Man and his dog's mission to rid the world of I.T. Woes, Worries & Peculiarities that affect your business...

First Printing, 2015
ISBN-13: 978-1519127808
ISBN-10: 1519127804

Published by B.S Net Limited T/A BrokenStones, providers of I.T. Support
& Consultancy to UK based Businesses - www.brokenstones.co.uk

Bridge House, Station Road, Lichfield, WS13 6HX
+44 (0) 1543 241016
http://chrisbluntbooks.co.uk

If you like this book…

Based on the fantastic feedback I get about the weekly E-mails that this book is based on, I'm confident you'll find this something of enormous use. I'd encourage you to be ruthless with this book, scribble all over and rip pages out when you find something useful. Don't be afraid!

If you like this book I'd be grateful if you'd post some positive feedback on Amazon or other book review sites, and of course feel free to share any comments on Facebook & twitter too.

You can also signup to the weekly mailing list that was the inspiration for the content in this book at http://chrisbluntbooks.co.uk/toptips/

I'd love to hear any feedback via http://facebook.com/brokenStonesIT or Twitter: @brokenStones

Acknowledgements

I'd like to thank all the readers of my weekly emails and all the fantastic feedback they've provided over the last year. I'm really passionate about seeing I.T. done properly, and making sure I.T. works for you, it's been amazing to see how my tips have helped so many.

An extra special mention to all those who have sent in specific questions that have provided ideas and content for these e-mails.

About the Author

Chris Blunt is owner and 'Head of Making things work' at brokenStones an I.T. support and Consultancy business in Lichfield, Staffordshire. Chris set up the business back in 2006 from a desire to make a difference to small businesses by providing IT services that are professional, dependable and cost effective.

His Key Technical Skills include Email Systems, Domains, Network Security and 'doing whatever it takes' to really get IT working for small businesses.

Graduating from Lancaster University in 2001 with a BSc Hons in Computer Science, Chris began his Professional IT career as a Software Programmer before seeing the opportunity to turn his hobby into a career and stepped into an IT Management role. It was during this time Chris started to develop his vision for brokenStones. Travelling all over the UK he saw many small businesses up-close and witnessed the poor level of IT services they were getting.

During his career Chris has worked for some of the world's largest organisations, such as Yahoo! along with some of the smallest one man bands... but his passion lies in helping owners of small and medium sized businesses *really* get their I.T. working for them.

To sum Chris up, he is one of the nicest guys you will ever meet, he is a true IT expert in every sense and he makes IT work for your business.

Chris is usually accompanied by his trusty Border collie, Donald, who is the most excitable and loveable dog you could ever hope to meet.
Just ignore his tongue sticking out, that's just his thing...

12 months of fun, serious and damn useful emails...PLUS a couple of extras on me...

Disclaimer

PLEASE NOTE: What you are about to read may cause you to question or worry about your own I.T. systems. I strongly urge you, if you have any concerns at all, to speak to your Local Trusted I.T. provider.

The following e-mails are designed to help you make better use of, and stay safe when using your computer. If you are at all unsure please ask an expert for advice, I make no warranties or accept any responsibility or liability for any adverse effects from following any of the advice in this book.

We rely on our I.T. Systems to run our businesses. When they break or go wrong it can cause us major problems. Don't leave these things to chance.

If you are at all unsure, don't have anyone to call, or you don't get an answer that you feel comfortable with then please,

Feel free to call my helpdesk on 01543 241 016.

We are available during normal UK business hours and are always eager to help. We will be able to give you quick and simple advice over the phone. If you need more in depth work doing will happily provide you with a list of services to suit your needs.

As Will Rogers said,

"Even if you're on the right track, you'll get run over if you just sit there"

From: Chris Blunt chrisblunt@brokenstones.co.uk

Sent: 22nd October 2015

Subject: **Introduction**

Hi,

Thanks for picking up my book, I hope you enjoyed the first volume and it helped with any issues you may have had.

If by chance you didn't read my first book, then feel free to hop on over to www.chrisbluntbooks.co.uk and grab yourself a copy.

The following pages share with you many useful tips and tricks I have discovered over the years to make the everyday problems of a business a little easier to manage.

These emails were sent every single week to members of an IT club to help avoid falling into the trap of online scams, to learn how to dispose of viruses quickly and safely and more importantly how to avoid these kind of things in the future.

They were written by me, a father of two, a dog lover and all over family man who loves his tech, to help other business men and women run their businesses with no i.t problems.

This book is 100% non-geeky and non-technical. It's just packed with golden, easy to understand I.T. tips that GUARANTEE business computers help your business rather than hinder it.

The emails are collectively a blueprint for IT peace-of-mind for any business owner with a computer (that they may sometimes want to throw out of the window – we've all been there!). Real life stories and feedback are all included to show the perils and delights of modern technology.

I've had so much great feedback over the last year from my I.T. Club members that it felt like a disservice to you if I didn't put the entire collection together in a book to share with everyone else.

This is my 12 month email diary.

This is as they got sent out. This is NOT the abridged version.

This is my advice.

I hope you enjoy, learn and remember a "Computer is for life, not just for Christmas"

Chris Blunt & Donald (the dog)

Top Tip:

Whenever you find a really useful tip, rip the page out... don't be afraid, I'm not going to come round and check to see if my book is still intact on your bookshelf, I'd be far prouder to see it being put to good use!

Rip the page out, scribble all over it and stick it up on your wall. If you are really precious and want a 'mint condition copy' drop me an email with a photo of what you've done to your current copy and I might just send you a signed version!

From: Chris Blunt chrisblunt@busstopgroup.co.uk

Sent: 27th February 2014

Subject: **I'm getting worried about all the complaints**

In the last few weeks I've seen the number of these **complaints go through the roof**.

I've had so **many people get in touch**, worried, including some who usually know better, its funny isn't it, if we get an email saying we've won something, most of us are sceptical and query if it's legitimate, but get an email saying we've done something wrong and we panic and want to find out more straight away...

I figured it was worth interrupting normal service and postponing the advertised topic this week to raise your awareness of this.

You will most likely have received an **email** recently claiming to be **from companies' house** and telling you **there has been a complaint** against your company.

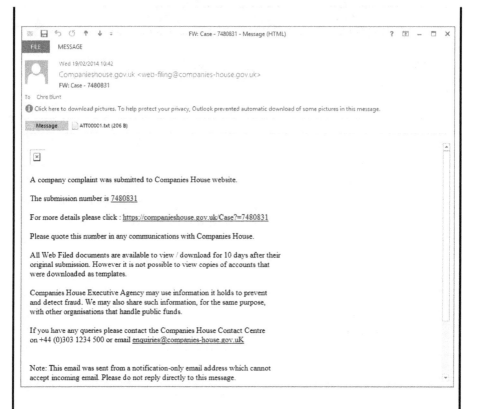

There hasn't, it's a scam, all designed to get you to click the link, which will then likely infect you with a virus, at best slowing your computer down, at worst costing you time, money and your business...

Now I'm going to repeat myself here, but there is one REALLY easy way to find out if **the email is a scam** and if you've been reading my emails for the last year (yes there has now been over 52 Top tips! *look out for my book soon!*) you will have heard this before...

Hover over the link (DON'T CLICK) and see what it says...

)laint was submitted to Companies House website.

umber is 7480831

http://wip.websiteexperts.com/carrots/index.html
Click to follow link

please click : https://companieshouse.gov.uk/Case?=7480831

number in any communications with Companies House.

As you can see, it's got nothing to do with company's house... and that means you need to treat the email with EXTREME caution...

So yes, this is a scam email currently going round, and it seems massive at the moment... In the last 7 days over 12,000 emails have passed through our filtering systems, over 5,700 of these have been detected and quarantined as spam, and a significant proportion of those emails have been 'Companies House Complaints'. I've also seen plenty of cases where it's not been picked up either... be careful, and extra vigilant...

Top Tip

I know I've said this many times before, but if you learn to make this a regular habit it will save your bacon one day...

Before you click ANY link in an email, hover over it and check out exactly where it's going to take you... if you are at all unsure, ask someone who knows...

For most of my I.T. life I've tried to dissuade people from cluttering up their desktop with loads of files and application short-cuts... but I never seem to get anywhere, if anything people seem to put MORE stuff on their desktop now... and that brings with it a little problem...

It's great having them all on your desktop, you know where they are and are really easy to get to... the trouble is when you are actually 'doing stuff', when you've got documents open, browsing the web, got your email open, running your accounts program... **you can't actually see them**.

Firstly I've got a really quick tip for 'peeking' at your desktop, if you just need to check if some things there...

Windows 7: WINDOWS KEY + Space Bar
Windows 8: WINDOWS KEY +, (comma)

This gives you a quick preview of your desktop, to be honest I don't use that shortcut very much myself, but the next one I do! A lot...

If you want to **jump back to your desktop** there is a really handy short-cut that I use a lot... it effectively **minimises all your open windows** in one swift key-press (well two! but who's counting)

WINDOWS + M - Minimise all open windows
(On the Mac it's Command + Option + M)

On a quick calculation, if you've got 4 windows open, it takes you at least 5 seconds to pick up the mouse, move it to the minimise button and click ... 4 times... so say you only need to get to your desktop once an hour, then over the course of a year this will save you over 2 and a half hours...

Top Tip

Keyboard short-cuts are all about saving you time, this is a great little one to learn if you often need to get back to stuff on your desktop...

WINDOWS KEY + M - Minimise all Open Windows

From: Chris Blunt chrisblunt@busstopgroup.co.uk

Sent: 13th March 2014

Subject: **The hidden space on your desktop**

I've seen quite a few people lately who have been **struggling with the size of their screen**, I'll be clear from the outset, this is NOT a discussion on the merits of different monitors and screen resolutions,

This is a **really quick tip** for you if you're **struggling** with a screen where you **can't quite see everything** you need to.

That's because there is a way to get a **little bit of extra space** for free, without changing your screen and without changing the resolution... I know a few people I've seen lately have found it **REALLY useful**, so I figured it worth sharing.

It involves **hiding the bar at the bottom of your screen** with the start button and open programs on (Windows calls it the Taskbar), when you are not using it quietly slides of the bottom of the screen, giving you an extra inch or so, then when you need it simply move you mouse to the very bottom of the screen and up it pops again...

On windows all you need to do is 'right click' on the taskbar and choose properties, then up pops this window and make sure 'Auto-Hid the taskbar' is ticked.

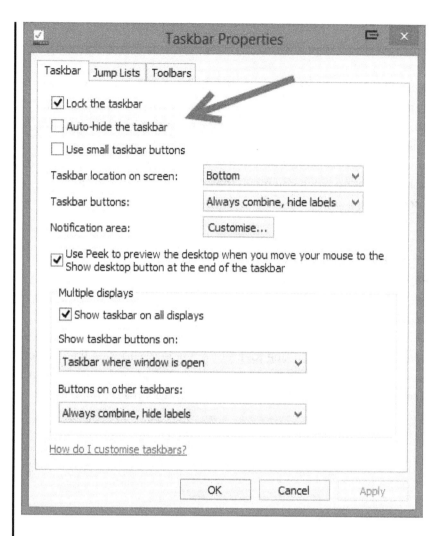

Then just click OK and you should find your taskbar slides neatly off the screen.

Now you'll find a little bit of extra room on your screen, which can make all the difference, and any time you need the taskbar just move your mouse to the very bottom of the screen and up it pops...

On the MAC, simply go to System Preferences > Dock and you'll find the option there (It's called the Dock on the mac), or press Command + Option + D.

Top Tip

If you are finding you can't quite see the 'OK/Cancel' buttons on some programs, or you could do with seeing just that *little bit more* off the bottom of your screen then try this little trick of hiding the task-bar, just right click on the taskbar, choose properties and then click 'Auto-Hide' now you've got an extra few Centimetres at the bottom of the screen and the task bar pops up when you move the mouse to the very bottom of your screen.

Have you got the right Screen?
It's not as straight forward as it might seem choosing the right computer screen, it's not the case that bigger is always better, and equally deciding to save a bit of money and get a smaller screen can also cause you a few problems with certain programs.

I've been thinking about putting together a "guide to choosing the perfect computer screen for you", is this something you'd find useful? Drop me a quick reply back and I'll get to work on it next week if the demand is there...

From: Chris Blunt chrisblunt@busstopgroup.co.uk

Sent: 20th March 2014

Subject: **At the risk of repeating myself**

So I messed up last week, but I think I got away with it as no-one seemed to notice...

What I promised I'd bring you this week, I realized I've already featured in a previous email... but as luck would have it I was having a conversation with someone about this very subject just a day later, so I know at least one person will find this super useful, and I don't doubt many more will too...

If you've read this before, and you've already got your phone backups set-up, good on you... if not have a read and I'd strongly advise you to get it sorted.

P.S. If you've got a question, or maybe even a tip of your own, send it in and I'll see what I can do to feature it!

How do you backup your iPhone?

Imagine if your entire phone got wiped today... have you got everything on their backed up? How quickly could you get back up and running again?

Cause if you've got an iPhone, and you've got iCloud backup set-up, it's minutes... even if you lose your phone, you can restore everything back to a new phone in minutes... I'm sure it's just as easy on an Android or Windows phone...

OK, so if you've got your email set-up properly (I.E. Office 365 or MS Exchange) then getting your Mail, Contacts and Calendar back is pretty easy, but what about all your settings, and all your apps, any notes you've made... re-downloading all your music and any photos you've taken?

I've got photos of Donald going back to when he was a puppy on my phone (yes and of course both my daughters too). The rest of the stuff on my phone I can either do without or get back with some effort, but I'd be pretty upset if I lost those precious photos.

Here's how we set-up Backup on your iPhone
(Note: These are from iOS 6, 7 is very similar, but I've not got it on my phone to show you!)

Go in to Settings and Choose 'iCloud'

Tap Settings on the Home Screen, then Tap iCloud

In the iCloud Menu scroll down to the bottom and choose 'Storage and Backup'

Now you're in the iCloud Menu, tap Storage and Backup to get to the backup options

The next screen tells you how much space you are using, and how much you have available, you then just need to make sure that 'iCloud Backup' is ON.

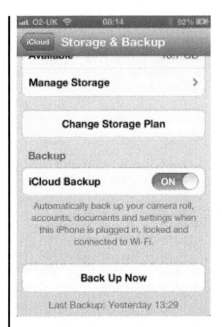

To enable iPhone Backup to iCloud just set iCloud Backup to on

Also just below the Back Up Now button it tells you when you last backed up... it's a simple as that... now whenever your phone has Wi-Fi and is plugged in it will automatically back itself up.

Side Note: Recently I ran out of space on my 'iCloud' I spent 2 or 3 weeks going through trying to delete stuff I didn't want / need... then I realized I was being pretty stupid! It was £28 to add an extra 20GB to my existing free 5GB, how much time had I already wasted? £28 for the year was nothing, it took less than a minute to set-up, and now I've got more space than I can use, and I've got peace of mind again...

Top Tip

Make sure you've got backup enabled on your phone right now, it's easy and it's free, and it all happens without you having to do anything! (You can also do the same thing on your iPad too!). I've not used a Samsung phone, but I'm sure it'll be just as simple, we've also got a new Windows Phone coming this week, so if you want help with that give us a call and we can talk you through it.

From: Chris Blunt chrisblunt@busstopgroup.co.uk

Sent: 27th March 2014

Subject: **Why SIZE really does matter**

I'll apologise in advance, I've had to inset of a bit techno-babble in to this email, I've tried to keep it as short and friendly as possible, but it was necessary in order to explain why Size really does matter, it is one of the most important factors when buying a new computer, but it's *the* thing which is overlooked almost every single time...

Screen Size

Think about it, what is the single thing you use most on your computer, whether it's a desktop or a laptop... what do you spend almost all of your time using... the screen, so why do most people not pay it a second thought when buying a new computer?

A bit of Background Techno-Babble...

I'm trying really hard here NOT to get too technical, but in relation to what we are talking about here there are two factors to bear in mind...

The physical screen size (That's like 15.6" or 22" or even 24")

Then there is the 'Resolution' which is basically how many little dots there are on the screen (this is represented like 1366x768 or 1920x1080 or 1920x1200)... the more dots the more you can see on the screen at any one time, but the smaller it will appear.

If you've got both a laptop and a desktop, try looking at a webpage on both of them (http://brokenstones.co.uk is a good one ;)) and you'll probably notice you can physically see more of the page on one than the other - this is because they are different resolutions...

OK, enough of the techno-babble, why does this matter?

Most people buy on screen size alone, going with the rule that bigger is better, but this isn't always the case. Because you get your lovely new screen and decide that the writing is a little too small, so you then go and lower the resolution, which makes everything bigger but means you see less on the screen and often distorts the picture

I've met quite a few people who say they don't like widescreen because it stretches their pictures...

- that's usually because the screen is set to the wrong resolution...

In actual fact you'd have been better off buying a slightly small screen with a lower natural resolution (i.e. it's more zoomed in!)

I'm afraid it gets more confusing than that when buying laptops too, take for instance the new laptop I've just got, that comes with a choice of THREE different screens, all the same physical size, but with different resolutions...

Top Tip

It's important that you get the right screen for you, one you feel comfortable with and one that you can see everything you need to without having to squint or lean forward to read the small bits!

The best advice I can give you if you are not sure about what the right screen is for you is to go and try some out... We've got a selection at our monthly IT clinics, and if there is a specific one you are looking at we can usually get a loan one in for you to try out... just email me back what you are looking for...

From: Chris Blunt chrisblunt@busstopgroup.co.uk

Sent: 3rd April 2014

Subject: **Did I leave my notebook there?**

Oddly, for an IT guy, I seem to use an awful lot of paper. I've got notepads for everything... and I'm always writing stuff down on scraps of paper...

The trouble is I'm always losing them, and it's a real pain when you can't find the one you want isn't it?

Can you relate to any other following?

Left your notebook behind at a client's?

Lost the notepad with 'that important note' in?

Know you've written something down but just can't find where?

Got a stack of notes, just don't know what to do with?

I used to suffer from some, if not all of those, and then a few months ago I started using something called 'Evernote'.

Evernote is basically an electronic notepad... but with a difference, it syncs across ALL your devices... so in a meeting I'll take notes on my iPad, and even whilst I'm still typing they are synced back to my desktop... and if I get home at night, and need to quickly check some notes from the day I can just check on my phone.

If you are like me and like to use a separate notepad for client meetings, vs Business development, that's easy, you can create multiple notebooks and store your notes in each one making it easy to find in the future. There's even a search box to quickly scour all your notes... now how much time have you wasted in the past flicking through notepad pages looking for that lost note?

You can even e-mail your notes straight out of Evernote so you can send the meeting minutes over before you've even left the room!

The best bit is, it's free...

Top Tip

Evernote is one of those tools which has changed the way I work, it's helped massively to cut down the amount of paper I get through, and it look far better sat in front of the client (especially for an IT guy!).

If you make a lot of notes, I'd urge you to give it a go –
(My link will give you 1 month of premium free, I find the free version is sufficient for my needs at the moment, so just skip the premium bit if you don't want it!)

Give away #1 – Free Month of EverNote Premium

I find EverNote a really useful tool, the standard version is completely free but the premium has a few extra bells and whistles. Use my link below to get your hands on a free month and see what you think for yourself.

http://chrisbluntbooks.co.uk/wsh2

From: Chris Blunt chrisblunt@busstopgroup.co.uk

Sent: 10th April 2014

Subject: **Have you bookmarked this?**

I'm going to be real quick about this one... because speed matters, and if you can do something quicker you can get more done.

This is so simple, it often gets over looked, I even find myself going through the same steps most weeks before I realise...

<< Test First Name >> Do you use bookmarks?

And do you use **'speed'** *bookmarks...*

Traditionally bookmarks have been used for pages you want to remember, but they are also mega useful for pages you visit often, especially when you use them as *'speed'* *bookmarks.*

By speed book marks I mean they are at the top level, really easy (and importantly QUICK) to get to... I use them for the web pages I visit multiple times a day, it saves me having to type in the address each time, I simply start a new Tab and click the page I want...

It's dead simple to do... here's how it works in Chrome - if you use a different browser, tell us on our https://www.facebook.com/brokenStonesIT and we'll send the instructions over for you...

When you are on the page you want, simply click the Star at the right side of the address bar

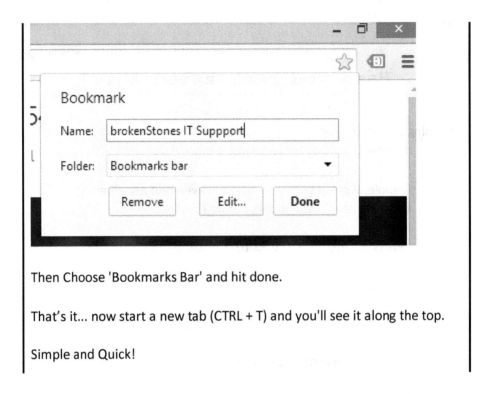

Then Choose 'Bookmarks Bar' and hit done.

That's it... now start a new tab (CTRL + T) and you'll see it along the top.

Simple and Quick!

Top Tip

If you've got web pages you visit two, three or more times a day, set-up a 'Speed Bookmark' for it... it *will* save you precious seconds that all add up at the end of the day!

From: Chris Blunt chrisblunt@busstopgroup.co.uk

Sent: 17th April 2014

Subject: **I tried to send you this**

I know I've mentioned this several times before, but unfortunately someone had this happen to them again recently...

It's exciting when we are expecting a delivery of something new isn't it? And then we go and miss it, either we're out, or in the garden, or just didn't hear the doorbell.

So when you get an email through from UPS with the tracking information on it's really tempting to go and click the link and see about getting it re-delivered.

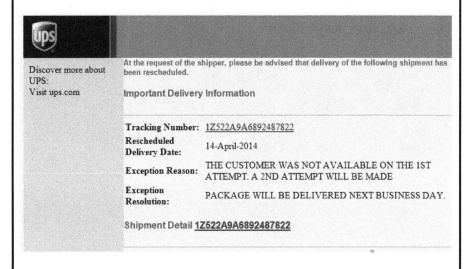

I see 3-4 of these caught by my own Spam filter each week, and if you hover over the link you'll see rather than take me to UPS, it's actually going to a rouge website.

Why?
It's hoping you'll click the link, and get infected with a virus, which will then allow them to capture some personal or banking details from you,

and generally cause havoc for you.

We often end up having to rebuild your computer if it gets one of these viruses, and you'll be looking at the best part of a day without your computer whilst we make sure everything is backed up, get all your software licenses, re-install it and put it back to how you like it.

Top Tip

This is probably the single best piece of advice I can give, I have said it many, many times over the course of the last year...

always, always, always... hover over any link before you click it... if it doesn't look right DON'T click it!

From: Chris Blunt chrisblunt@busstopgroup.co.uk

Sent: 24th April 2014

Subject: **Your domain is up for renewal**

We all get quite worried about losing our domain names. Just imagine how much faff you'd have to go through to **change you email address**, website etc. if you forgot to renew it...

Frankly **I'm surprised there are not more Domain Name Renewal Scams** out there, the BIG one I've written about several times the 'Domain Registry of America', I know **several people who have fallen victim** to that.

So I was intrigued to see **a new one** come through to me last week, what do you think?

Thu 10/04/2014 13:49

Domain Services <admin@instantservicesnetwork.com>

Domain Notification: CHRIS BLUNT This is your Final Notice of Domain Listing - BUSSTOPGROUP.COM

To ☐ Chris Blunt

Attention: Important Notice

Complete and return by fax to:
1-716-242-0405

DOMAIN SERVICE NOTICE

ATT: CHRIS BLUNT
ADMINISTRATIVE CONTACT
BROKENSTONES LIMITED
▓▓▓▓▓▓▓▓▓ROKENSTONES.NET%
BRIDGE HOUSE STATION ROAD - - LICHFIELD - STAFFORDSHIRE -
UNITED KINGDOM
WWW.BUSSTOPGROUP.COM
Please ensure that your contact information is correct or make the
necessary changes above

Domain Name:

BUSSTOPGROUP.COM

Search Engine Submission

Requested Reply
APRIL 10,2014

PART I: REVIEW SOLICITATION

Attn:
As a courtesy to domain name holders, we are sending you this notification for your business
Domain name search engine registration. This letter is to inform you that it's time to send in your
registration and save.

Failure to complete your Domain name search engine registration by the expiration date may result
in cancellation of this offer making it difficult for your customers to locate you on the web.

Privatization allows the consumer a choice when registering. Search engine subscription includes
domain name search engine submission. You are under no obligation to pay the amounts stated
below unless you accept this offer. Do not discard, this notice is not an invoice it is a courtesy
reminder to register your domain name search engine listing so your customers can locate you on
the web.

This Notice for: WWW.BUSSTOPGROUP.COM will expire on APRIL 10,2013 Act today!

DETAIL OF SERVICE: ANNUAL WEBSITE SEARCH ENGINE SUBMISSION FOR DOMAIN NAME WWW.BUSSTOPGROUP.COM

Detail of Service:	Reply by Date:		For Domain Name:
SEARCH SUBMISSIONS	04/10/2014		BUSSTOPGROUP.COM

Domain Services No items   ∧

It's made up to look, at first glance, like a renewal for your domain name, but if you look a little closer **it's actually talking about "search engine submission"**... Take it from me, this is **utter rubbish**, I'm not going to go in to the why's and wherefores of this particular scam, but just to say if you have any search engine submission queries talk to your Web Guy (or Girl).

I particularly like the small print on this E-mail, I've highlighted a couple of my favourites below...

"Note that THIS IS NOT A BILL. This is a solicitation."

"This notice is not in any part associated with a continuation of services for domain registration."

And then **this little beauty** too...

"...Search engine submission is an optional service that you can use as a part of your website optimization and alone may not increase the traffic to your site..."

Great, So what they've said in the 'small print' in summary is although this may look like an invoice, it's not **we're just touting for your business**, it's got **nothing to do with the renewal** of your domain name, oh and what we are trying to sell you probably **won't actually make any difference** to your website anyway...

Top Tip

Renewing your domain name *should* cost you around **£10 a year**, and you should recognize the people asking you to renew (i.e. the same as last year!). Yes, it's important to **keep your domain name renewed**, but be wary of anything you don't recognize and if you are in any doubt call someone in the know about Domain Names... like me!

From: Chris Blunt chrisblunt@busstopgroup.co.uk

Sent: 1ˢᵗ May 2014

Subject: **How did you get my details?**

If you run your own business, the chances are at some-point you are going to need to send a letter to someone who's address you don't know.

I've spoken to 6 or 7 people in the last couple of months who've all wanted to do this, and it's really stumped them... they've spent a not insignificant amount of time trying to find out their address and failed...

So it came as a bit of a surprise to them when I found it out in 5 of the cases in about 7 seconds...

There's a little trick us 'IT Guys' have for finding out where you live... it doesn't involve any covert operations, private detectives or MI5 secret stuff... all you need is their email address and it's freely available information.

You see if your domain name is registered properly it should have you own, or your companies name and Address listed against it. (And if it doesn't you really should sort that out, it's one of the few ways you've got of proving you own your own domain!)

Now I've raised 3 points here, which I don't really like to do in one e-mail, so let's deal with them really quickly...

1. I've talked in previous Top Tips about how important it is to **check you do actually own your own domain name**, so all I'll say is if you don't see your own name when you check your domain name get that sorted ASAP. **Ask me if you want more info.**

2. If you are not happy about your personal details appearing on your domain name there is something called 'domain privacy' which you can enable on all non-UK domains, expect to pay about £5 a year for the service. **Ask me if you want more info.**

3. My original point to this e-mail, it's a really great, quick check to see if you can find out someone's address... you do need to treat it with a pinch of salt as it may be out of date, but like I said it takes about 7 seconds and is a whole lot quicker than searching websites and directories for them...

Top Tip

It's a two-parter this week...
a. Make sure your own details are correct on your domain name, run the who is tool and check it's you that's named on your domain name, and not your web provider or someone completely different!
b. It sounds a bit stalker-esk, but checking someone's domain name is a great place to start if you're looking for their contact details...

Give away #2 – Do you own your domain?

Use this free domain checker to find out who is actually listed as the owner of your domain name.

http://chrisbluntbooks.co.uk/wsh2

From: Chris Blunt chrisblunt@busstopgroup.co.uk

Sent: 8th May 2014

Subject: **Where your passwords are stored...**

If you use **Google Chrome**, or have ever used Google Chrome, you will probably want to take note of this.

I had a phone call from a very good friend of mine, he was about hand his laptop back to his employer and wanted to know if there was **anything he should be doing to remove personal information before he handed it back**.

And that got me thinking, because there are a few things you should attend to, but Google Chrome is probably the most important thing... for me it's got **one massive security floor**, that if you're ever going to hand your computer over to someone you need to think seriously about...

As you know, usually when you login to a website it pops up and asks if you want to remember your password for next time... which is really handy and saves you having to remember loads of passwords right...

Well here is the **scary thing**, if you know your computer password **you can see ALL of those passwords** that you've saved...

Try it for yourself now... try putting 'chrome://settings/passwords' in to the address bar in chrome, you should see something like this pop up...

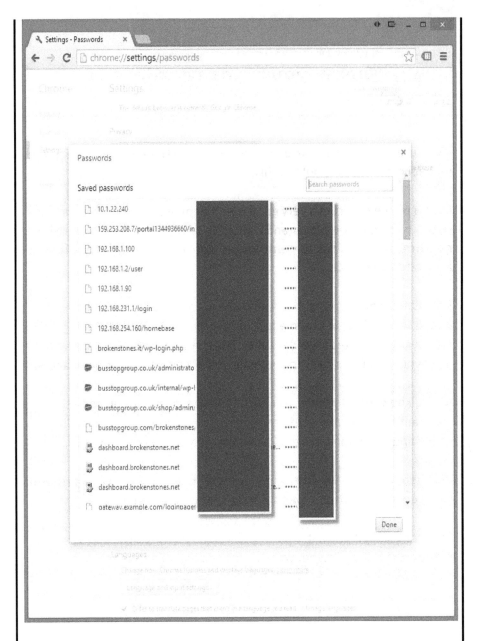

Now click on the dots on the right hand side, and you'll see a little 'Show' box pop up, if you click the Show button it'll ask for your computer password (If you've got one!).

There you go, anyone who knows your computer password can now see

ALL of the passwords you've got stored in Google Chrome...

The truth is both Firefox and Internet Explorer also do this, although Firefox does have a 'master password' option to give an extra level of protection.

The simple answer is, if you are ever handing your computer over to someone you don't completely trust, it's a really good idea to clear your browser history...

I've gone on for enough today, so I've put together a handy little download guide showing you how to clear your password and other browsing history in the main browsers –

Top Tip

Your computer collects a lot of private information about you, and is VERY good at collecting passwords to make it easy for you to login to the plethora of websites you need to access on a daily basis, but just think about this information if you have to hand your computer over to a 3rd party...

Again I've got a two-parter for you this week...

a. **Use an I.T. provider you REALLY trust**, when you turn your computer over to us, we've pretty much got access to your entire life.

b. If you ever have to hand your computer over to someone you don't implicitly trust then **clear out all of your password and browsing history** (grab my guide on how to do that here:

From: Chris Blunt chrisblunt@busstopgroup.co.uk

Sent: 15th May 2014

Subject: **RE: Check Data**

I'm taking a break from the norm this week, as you know I usually try to be as broad as possible with my tips, so it's relevant to the majority of everyone that reads them.

But this is so vitally important I figured it was still worth sharing, if it's not directly relevant to you, please accept my apologies, you will undoubtedly know someone who this is relevant to, pass it on to them.

If you don't use sage, or know anyone that does you might as well skip to the bottom of this email (Just hit the END key now).

If you use Sage Accounts you REALLY need to read and take note of this.

In the last 2 weeks I've had to get involved 3 times to repair peoples accounts data because they didn't follow these guidelines.

There is a process in sage called '**Check Data**' it's a process that runs and checks for errors, inconsistencies and corruptions. You usually get prompted for this j**ust before you run a backup**.

I run Check Data every day, at the same time I do a backup. (You do run Sage Backup don't you? - it's a separate process to your normal nightly backups!)

Here's the really important bit, **if you EVER get an error**, even just one, you need to stop, **stop and get it fixed** BEFORE you keep on working.

In the best cases it's taken me around an hour to get the errors fixed, in the worst cases (Usually where the errors have been ignored for several weeks / months) it's taken several days and £000's to get it fixed, if at all.

The reason you need to stop straight away is if it turns out the errors can't be fixed (and I have seen some examples of this), you will have to restore from your last good backup, and if that was several weeks / months ago, you are going to have an awful lot of information to re-enter!

Top Tip

If you use Sage Accounts you should be running Check Data on a regular basis (along with your backups).

If Check Data EVER shows an error, you MUST get it fixed ASAP, and BEFORE you keep on working in Sage.

Again my apologies if you don't use Sage, but someone you know probably does, and they'll thank you for sharing this with them.

From: Chris Blunt chrisblunt@busstopgroup.co.uk

Sent: 22nd May 2014

Subject: **Is it a bit hairy?**

You'll probably remember the old fashioned 'Ball' Mouse, how frustrating it was when the mouse would jump all over the screen and no matter how hard you tried getting it on to the point you wanted, it just didn't happen...

They were always getting clogged up with dirt and dust and you were forever having to taken the apart to clean them...

If you were like me, you'd drop the ball out the bottom and move the rollers yourself... oh and then there would be the time you'd come back from holiday to find out some joker had been and nicked your Mouse ball!

The advent of the 'Ball-less' optical mouse changed all of this, and we quickly got used to vastly improved accuracy and smooth tracking... but this has brought its own problems, because they are more accurate the 'target' for us to click on has got smaller... which is fine most of the time, but **do you sometimes find that your mouse still jumps around**?

Especially if you've eaten your lunch at your desk that day? (Or maybe I'm just a messy eater!)

One of my own team had exactly this problem the other day, their mouse was jumping all over the place and it was pretty frustrating to try and use it. It had been doing it for a few weeks apparently and they'd had enough.

If you're getting this problem yourself, then here's a little trick, this is what I did, it's quite a common problem and it's a REALLY simple fix...

Flip your mouse upside down, and where the sensor it, give it a good blow... that's it... you might feel a bit silly, but trust me it works, next time your mouse starts jumping around try it...

What you often find it a single hair has got stuck in the sensor and that's causing the jumping around... it certainly was in our case, and the mouse was good as new...

Top Tip

If you're finding your mouse doesn't track as smoothly as it used too, and jumps around the screen a bit, **check the sensor is clear of debris**, you will often find a single human hair stuck in the sensor. Also if you've got a standard Optical mouse make sure your desk is not 'too shiny' - The Optical Mouse needs a good patterned surface to work best on.

Myself I swear by the Logitech Darkfield Mouse's, I've used them for about 4-5 years now and the performance is just outstanding... When you just want it to work perfectly every-time it's one of the best out there.

From: Chris Blunt chrisblunt@busstopgroup.co.uk

Sent: 29th May 2014

Subject: **Have you forgotten something?**

UBER BORING FACT ALERT! The number one thing most overlooked thing people forget when buying a new computer... PLUS - **How to get a new computer for free**...

I was talking to someone just this morning, they'd bought a lovely new computer a few months ago (from your local national Computer Store), recently the DVD Drive has packed up... it's been fixed once already and has just broken again... he can't face the prospect of sending it off a 2nd time and waiting for a week or more for it to be returned...

As I started talking about a few of the features he should look for in a warranty (*Yea, my conversations can be THAT exciting!!*) I think he started to realise it'd be good to chat with me before rushing out to buy a new computer next time! (Partly My fault - I hadn't told him **we also sell computers!!** - BONUS TIP BELOW)

The last thing you want to think about when buying a new computer is what happens if it goes bang isn't it? Which I guess is why most people just settle for 'as it comes' when it comes to a Warranty... but it can actually be the most valuable item to buy... (I would say 'worth its weight in gold'.... but as they are mostly electronic now that's not saying much!)

Let me put it this way, on several occasions in the last year I've known incidents where a 3 - 5 year old computer has literally gone 'pop' (yes even smoke in one case!), and off the back of that they've got a BRAND NEW, up to date computer out of it.

My Pet Hate
One of my Pet Hates is when I come across companies which have been sold custom built computers by an independent computer company, you are then effectively tied to that company for the life of that computer if you want to keep the warranty. You are far better insisting on a reputable

brand (my two favourites are HP & Dell) and ensuring the warranty is 'Manufacturer Backed', that way if you fall out with the independent (or they go out of business!) you can still refer back to the manufacturer.

Aren't they just a waste of money / Money Making Scam / Extra Tax

Of course it depends who / where you get it from, but generally if you've got a reputable Manufacturer backed warranty, then No.

It'll cover any kind of hardware failure with your computer, parts and usually the labour too.

Remember, a warranty is basically an insurance policy, just in case something goes wrong... it's not I.T. Support cover (you should have that as well!)

Top Tip

Whenever you are buying a new computer always get a minimum of a 3 year, Next Business Day, On Site Warranty, Backed by the Manufacturer...

Three Warranty Factors to consider:

Make sure you've got a **manufacturer backed** warranty, not just one from Any Old Company

Do you need an *onsite Warranty?* Or would you be happy to send your computer off and wait for a week or two for it to be sent back?

The Warranty generally covers the *Hardware* only, you need to take care of your Software Licenses and Data. (Or get a good I.T. Company to look after this for you!)

BONUS TIP

Even it if seems obvious, tell people what you do... the person I mentioned above knew we did I.T. support, but not that we sold computers!! I could have saved him a whole world of pain...

Giveaway #3 - Free Warranty Check Service

Take advantage of our free warranty check service and find out what type of warranty you have and how long is left.

http://Chrisbluntbook.co.uk/wsh2

From: Chris Blunt chrisblunt@busstopgroup.co.uk

Sent: 5th June 2014

Subject: **Have Internet, Will Travel**

I've got a lot on this week, so I'll keep this really brief, if you find yourself out and about a lot like me, and you're constantly trying to jump on the Hotel's Free Wi-Fi, or get connected to your customers Wi-Fi, then I've got the perfect answer for you.

It's dug me out of a hole on many occasions, when you've got something urgent you need to jump on-line quickly for, or you've been promised an internet connection where you're going to, only to get there an find out it doesn't work, or is just painfully slow...

That's why I always carry my 4G Dongle around with me, it's basically mobile internet access and it somehow manages to get internet access in places I can barely get a signal on my mobile phone!

For example I was in Wales last week, we could barely get a TV Signal, let alone Mobile Signal... most of my phone calls cut out half way through and had to be repeated... yet with my 4G dongle I could still get all my emails, login to my CRM System, my Wife did the Sainsbury's shopping and it was all quite painless.

For me, being out and about a lot and pretty dependant on the internet for a lot of what I do £15 is a no-brainer. Sure you can use your mobile phone as a Wi-Fi Hotspot, but in my experience you don't get as good performance, and it cuts you off if you make a phone call.

Top Tip

If you spend a lot of the time out and about (or perhaps just wanting to work outside over the summer!) think about investing in a decent 4G dongle, they just make getting on line really easy.

I just know this is going to be a bit controversial... and the amount of times I get asked about this I REALLY should have mention this before now...

Should you leave your computer on overnight, or should you turn it off?

There are two schools of thought on this one, if you want to be 100% as energy efficient as you can then you'll probably turn it off... but if you are like me and don't want to wait the extra few seconds in the morning then you'll probably leave it on... I'll be honest with you I would simply not remember to turn it off every night even if I wanted too...

Whichever way you want to go, **there is something far better you can do first**... and that's make sure you've got Power Saving mode set-up correctly...

This handily puts your computer to 'sleep' when it detects you've not used it for a specified amount of time, I have mine set so after 10 minutes my monitor turns off, and after 30 minutes my computer goes to sleep... to wake it up I simply wiggle the mouse or tap the keyboard and within a couple of seconds it's back to where I left it...

Power Saving has the added benefit that when you are called away from your desk, or even on a long phone call your computer will automatically 'go to sleep'... only to resume from exactly where you left off when you wake it up again...

You can check and set-up your power saving mode by going in to Control Panel and choosing '**Power Options**' and then hitting '**Change Plan Settings**' (**On the Mac** go to System Preferences and Choose 'Energy Saver' - if you've got a laptop you can also decide what to do when you close the lid and have different settings depend on whether you are on battery or plugged in!

QUICK TIP ALERT: If you use Windows 8 simply press WINDOWS KEY + X and you'll pop up a quick menu with a link to Control Panel.

QUICK TIP ALERT 2: Especially useful on Laptops, choose what to do when you press the power button - I have mine set so when I close the lid it goes to sleep and when I press the power button it shuts down.

Top Tip

Customising your power saving settings, and getting your power button doing what you want is one of those things that just makes life that little bit easier... doubly so if you've got a laptop..

Regardless of whether you prefer to always shut your computer down or always leave it on... take 5 minutes today to check your power saving settings and check it's how you want it to be...

From: Chris Blunt chrisblunt@busstopgroup.co.uk

Sent: 23rd June 2014

Subject: **What happened whilst I was off ill?**

For the first time in 70 weeks there was no Top Tip last week, thank you too all of you who e-mailed to check if everything was OK.

As you know I write these fresh every week, and last week I was ill, so ill I couldn't even face lifting my head of the pillow to write you an e-mail. Sorry.

But you know what, a strange thing happened whilst I was at home tucked up in bed battling with a 40 degree temperature... everything kept on working (well expect my weekly emails!!)

I mean the business kept on running, nothing ground to a halt, my staff were able to deal with my important e-mails and my office manager re-arranged all my diary appointments... I had almost zero input last week...

So as a bonus here's something a little bit different, a thinking point for you... would the same be true in your business? If you were suddenly off for a week from today, with no notice and no time to prepare anything, would everything keep ticking along?

Even if it's just you in your business there are still things you can do to help with this, and of course having the right I.T. systems in place helps massively with this too.

So I know it's not strictly I.T. related, but I thought it a useful thing to stimulate your thinking, normal service will be resumed on Thursday...

Top Tip

This Thursday: A Killer Keyboard Shortcut...

From: Chris Blunt chrisblunt@busstopgroup.co.uk

Sent: 26th June 2014
Subject: **The Three Fingered Kill**

Do you know what, I've just looked at what I was going to talk to you about this week, and I've really struggled to find a reason as to why / how that would help you... so I'm throwing that out of the window and instead I've got three really quick, really useful Keyboard short-cuts for you.

Re-Opening a Closed Tab
I'm always doing this, closing the wrong tab in my web browser, then you have to open up a new tab, search for that page again and get back to where you were...
NO, just hit **CTRL + SHIFT + T** and it'll open up your last closed Tab - Works in Chrome, IE & Firefox.

Lock Your Computer
Stepping away from your computer for a few moments, just hit **WINDOWS + L** to lock it and stop anyway prying at your stuff. *(In our office if you leave your computer unlocked, you usually get back to find you have kindly emailed everyone offering to buy them a drink that evening)*

Close a Program / Window
Quickly close a program or window without having to fiddle with the mouse *(Especially useful on laptops when you're using the track pad!)* - **ALT + F4** will close your current highlighted program or window.

Top Tip

Getting to know your keyboard short-cuts can save you a whole heap of time, look at the things you do most with your mouse, and find out how to do them with your keyboard instead...

Re-Open a Closed Web Browser Tab - **CTRL + SHIFT + T**
Lock your Computer - **WINDOWS + L**
close the current program / window - **ALT + F4**

Subject: **It's a personal thing**

I'm sorry, I'm a little bit conscious I've been neglecting something lately, I've talked a lot about the power of the keyboard short-cut, and it's almost felt like I've been trying to persuade you against using a mouse at all.

But that's not fair, because using right your mouse can be just as powerful.

Let me say this right from the start, **there is nothing wrong with the standard 2 button optical scroll mouse that comes with most new computers now**. Although it is somewhat limiting when it comes to getting the most out of your computer.

There is a lot to be said for getting yourself a decent 'keeper' mouse... one you find super comfortable to use, and makes life that bit easier day to day...

There are two key features you should look for in a mouse that save you a bucket load of time all day, every day...

1. A Scroll wheel - Most new machines come with a scroll wheel mouse now. Believe it or not, I meet a lot of people who don't know how to use it! Whenever you see the scroll bar at the right hand side of the screen, just use the wheel to move the page up and down... I use it most in my web browser and in Word...

2. Back & Forward Buttons - These handy little buttons let you go back and forward in your web browser, it saves you having to move up to the top of the screen and click back the whole time.

Both of these features although small, will save a couple of seconds each time, but you'd be surprised just how much you use them every day.

Its Personal

Choosing the right mouse is a personal thing, you need to find something you are comfortable using, and that you find easy to use, I've done just that with the Logitech Performance MX, I've had it for almost 5 years now and it's pretty much the best mouse I've ever used.

Why? Well first and foremost, it works reliably, I find it really comfortable to use and the buttons are really intuitively placed... And the buttons are where this mouse really excels... I'm not going to bore you with all the details, but one thing that really makes this mouse special is the Thumb button, you can customize it to do pretty much what you want... mine pops up my screen capture software, something I use a lot, and something that saves me a lot of time.

Top Tip

Like I said, there is nothing wrong with the stock mouse that ships with most new computers now, but if you are in to making things that bit easier for yourself, and looking out for every opportunity to save yourself a bit of extra time, then getting yourself a decent mouse is a good investment.

Subject: **I'm a bit pinned down**

Here's something I come across a lot that loads of **people are not taking advantage** of.

If you've got programs you use a lot, it make sense to **make them really easy to access** right? So when you need them it's **super easy quick to open** them up?

The way I see most people do this is by dropping a short-cut on their desktop. But then to get to it you need to minimise all your open windows, and find it on your desktop (which is usually pretty cluttered!)

So here's a little tip... **Pin it to your Task Bar...**

Then you'll never need to minimise anything, it's always there sat on the taskbar, ready and waiting for you...

Here's how

Find the program you want, either on your desktop or start menu / screen and simply **right click**... there you'll see a '*Pin to Taskbar*' option, click this and it'll magically appear on our taskbar at the bottom of the screen.

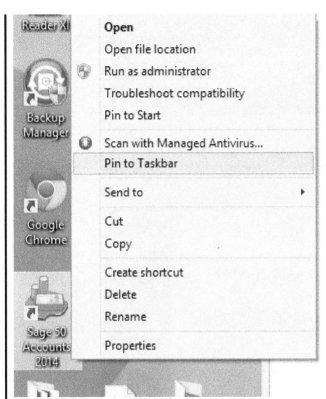

If your program is on the desktop, this is what it looks like.

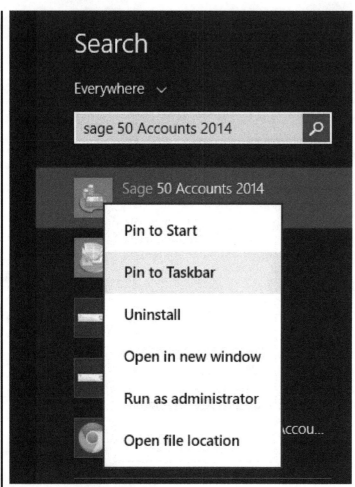

If you're on Windows 8, just hit start and type the program you want, then right click like above.

Now all you need to do is click the icon on the taskbar and up pops the program.

Here's **one last trick** for taskbar icons... some programs have **'secret' shortcuts** once you've pinned them to your taskbar...

Google Chrome and Internet Explorer are prime examples of this, just right click on them on the taskbar and notice some extra options...

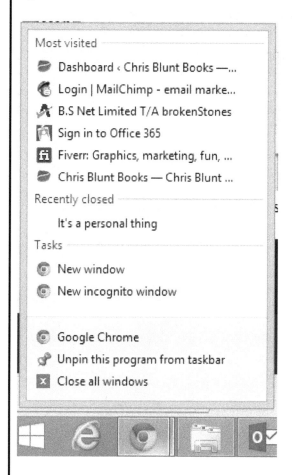

Notice as well as being able to open up your recent and most visited pages you can also create a new window, or something I use a lot an 'incognito Window'

Top Tip

Look at what programs you use most day to day, the ones you are always having to click start, or search for on your desktop... then **pin them to your taskbar**... the few seconds it saves you each time will add up massively over the year...

From: Chris Blunt chrisblunt@busstopgroup.co.uk

Sent: 17th July 2014

Subject: **How to make your laptop explode**

A common bug bear I hear with Laptops is how the battery never seems to last that long, when I sit down and chat with people about this, I usually hear a common story, if you're sat next to a plug socket, the laptops usually plugged in... And here is where I believe the issue lies...

Some people think that by leaving their laptop plugged in the whole time they are saving the life of their battery, but the opposite tends to be true, the less you use the battery, the less effective it will become.

The advice I tend to give out to laptop users is to NOT leave your laptop plugged in the whole time, but to unplug it once it's charged, to use the battery and then to plug it back in when it gets low again.

A modern laptop should give you minimum of 4 hours (I get 6-7 from my new one), and if you look after the battery properly it should last for at least 2-3 years.

I speak from personal experience, I used to use my laptop on the train every single day for 18 months, I'd get a good 4-5 hours from it every day, then I'd charge it up at home every night. Then I stopped travelling on the train, and my laptop stayed plugged in pretty much constantly for 3 months. The next time I took it out it died within 15 minutes, and that was it, the battery would not run the laptop for more than 10-15 minutes after that.

It's not just me either...
Apple even recommends 'Keeping the electrons moving' (https://www.apple.com/uk/batteries/notebooks.html) saying you **should not leave your laptop plugged in all the while**, and the 'ideal user' is someone who uses their laptop on the train on the way to work, and then plugs in at the office to charge.

It might explode

Another warning, only use the official manufacturer chargers, and make sure you use the RIGHT charger for your laptop. Below is a picture of what happened to one of our clients laptops when they used the wrong charger.

As you can see the outside of the (metal!) case is all buckled where the laptop EXPLODED inside... They thought they were saving £30 by getting a cheaper charger, but ended up having to buy a whole new laptop. Whoops.

Top Tip

To get the most out of your battery life, unplug your laptop once it's fully charged. Don't leave it plugged in 24x7.

Don't leave your laptop plugged in all the time, once it's charged unplug it.

Always use the correct charger as recommended by the manufacturer.

From: Chris Blunt chrisblunt@busstopgroup.co.uk

Sent: 24th July 2014

Subject: **What's the best number to contact you on?**

Have you ever noticed how many people send you an email without a phone number at the bottom? Or worse don't even include their name / company details at the bottom?

It's crazy because it's so, so simple to make sure each and every email has this on, but I'm still amazed and bamboozled by the number of people that e-mail me and don't include any contact details to call them on...

I know I'm an 'IT Guy' and I should be making use of modern technology, but a lot of the time it's just easier and quicker to pick up the phone... and that's the point of modern technology right? To make things easier and quicker...

Yes you should have a wonderful CRM system that stores all the contact details, and yes you can quickly search on the web... but why put an extra barrier between someone getting in touch with you?

It's another of the things that really annoy me, and it's a shame because it's so easy to do just by setting up your e-mail signature correctly...

Rather than write another lengthy e-mail, I've put together exactly how to do this in a handy little PDF guide for you,
It's not just your main e-mail client either, make sure you've set your email signature up on your phone, iPad and anywhere else you regularly send email from... if you'd like help with any of these, just drop a message on to our Facebook page
- http://www.facebook.com/brokenStonesIT and we'll send you a link with how to do it.

So, how difficult is it to find the right phone number to call you on?

Oh, and I thought I'd best just double check everywhere I send email from...I'd best go set-up my e-mail signature on my iPad... what devices have you forgotten?

Check you've got your E-Mail signature setup correctly... I've got two types set on my computer, 1 for 'New E-Mails' which has my full details on, and one for Replies, which is a bit shorter and just has the basics on (including my phone number!).

I've also got it setup on my iPhone, and [now] my iPad too...

Giveaway #4 – Professional email signature

Grab my free PDF guide on how to configure your email signature in Microsoft outlook.

http://chrisbluntbooks.co.uk/wsh2

From: Chris Blunt chrisblunt@busstopgroup.co.uk

Sent: 31st July 2014

Subject: I've got the usual brush off again...

Ok, so it's probably the biggest joke of the I.T. world... "Have you rebooted your computer?" and thanks to TV shows like 'The IT Crowd' it's seen as a way to get you off the phone and a waste of time.

But it's not, there is a genuine reason and some science behind it. I'm not going to go in to detail on that, but look at it this way...

Our job as your I.T. support is to get the problem fixed as quickly and efficiently for you.

There is nothing we would love more than to spend a few hours tracing a particular problem and working out exactly what's happened and why. But if there is a good chance that can be fixed in 5 minutes with a quick Turn it off and turn it back on again then that makes far more sense doesn't it?

Now clearly if you are having to do this every day there is a more serious, underlying issue that really should be looked in to, but as a one off the odd reboot does the world of good, and it's not just a brush off because we're busy!

Top Tip

As Cliché as it sounds, when something's not working and you're not quite sure what's gone wrong when a quick reboot of your computer can often sort the issue out for you. If you are at all worried, or it's happening on a regular basis then you should really get it checked out.

From: Chris Blunt chrisblunt@busstopgroup.co.uk

Sent: 7th August 2014
Subject: **I've behaved a bit like a monkey**

Last week was my birthday, and as has been tradition since the age of 5 I have my friends round for a party... The format has remained pretty much the same for almost 30 years, we do some kind of activity, eat too much food, and drink far too many fizzy drinks.

This year for the activity part we went to 'Go Ape', the thing where you climb up a tree and then jump and swing through the forest. (*Now you should understand at this point I REALLY don't like heights... but I'm into stepping out of my comfort zone at the moment, so it seemed a good thing to take on.*)

Now ordinarily this would be quite a dangerous thing to do, run across a balance beam 30 feet up, jump between wooden planks secured by nothing more than 2 pieces of rope, or even swing out a tree in to a cargo net. But they've got some really good safety systems that vastly reduce this danger...

In the I.T. world we'd call these 'Backups', the safety ropes to catch your business by if something goes wrong... And I think there are a few lessons to take away from how Go Ape run things...

Firstly the safety system (or 'backup system') is designed in such a way that you are NEVER not attached, and at the really risky places you actually have 3 safety lines. But the most important aspect to me, and the side that most businesses let themselves down on was someone checking things were working right...

It's all good and well having a good backup system in place, but if you're not checking its working, and things are working like they are supposed to then you're exposing yourself to a big risk.

You see all round the forest there are staff there checking the safety systems are in good condition and are being used correctly. Most businesses I come across either don't or only have a very poor system for checking their backups are actually protecting them.

3/4 of the way round the guy in the tree next to me was about to un-clip himself completely from the safety line, but as he was about to a shout came out from one of the marshals for him to stop, and think about what he was doing.

Now I may have turned this in to a bit of a story, just to tell you all about my adventure swinging through the trees, but it's really important message behind it... It's one thing having backups, but it's a much more important task to be checking they are actually working and being used correctly.

Top Tip

I've said it before, and I will undoubtedly come across the same mistakes in the future...
Here's a few questions to ask yourself, and if any of the answers make you feel uncomfortable then maybe you should do something about them.

Who checks your backups are working correctly?

How do YOU know your backups are working correctly?

When did YOU last check your backups worked?

Do you get an email when your backups fail? (Do you get one when they work?)

When did you last do a test restore to make sure you can recover from your backups?

Don't just set-up your backups and forget about them... check they are working, regularly.

From: Chris Blunt chrisblunt@busstopgroup.co.uk

Sent: 14th August 2014

Subject: **Giving it the middle finger**

I'm going to start off with an Apology, it's easy to overlook some things that are just so natural to you, and **I kind of assumed this was just a given**, but after having gone through this with several people in the last few weeks I figured it was worth a quick mention here...

So please accept my apologies if either you've been missing out for the last 18 months or this is second nature to you... I promise I'll keep this one short for you.

As you'll have gathered by now, **it frustrates me when I see people not making the most of their IT systems**, when they are doing things 'the long way round'... so **what do you do with your middle finger** when your browsing the web?

What I've noticed is quite a few people don't really understand what the Mouse Wheel is for...

I see so many people using the scroll bars at the side of the screen rather than just giving the wheel a little spin with their middle finger...

Any time you see a scroll bar at the right hand side of the screen you can usually push your mouse wheel up or down to move up and down the page... you don't have to hover over the ever shrinking up / down arrows and click... just use the wheel, once you've used it a few times you'll wonder how you ever lived without it...

If you've got a decent mouse, you might also find the wheel tilts left and right so you can scroll sideways too... (Very hand in Excel!!)

I could go on, but I promised I'd keep this one short and simple...

Learning all the little short-cuts make a real difference and save your precious seconds that actually mount up to a whole heap of saved time...

If you've not already using your mouse wheel, start. Practice scrolling up and down a web page or a word document... it does make life much easier.

If you are already using your mouse wheel, find out what else it can do... some mouse wheels also act as a 3rd button which you can program to do stuff (like zoom in / out, open up a web browser / copy or paste).

Giveaway #5 – Ask a Question

As you'll have noticed, a lot of my e-mails are in direct response to questions my readers have sent in... If you've got a question of your own hop over to our Facebook page and post the question

http://facebook.com/brokenstonesIT

Or if you'd rather not share it publicly send it direct to me here:

http://chrisbluntbooks.co.uk/wsh2

We've been setting up a lot of new email accounts for people lately, and I've been finding a lot of confusion out there around e-mail addresses, specifically the different types and what you can / can't have.

So at the risk of getting technical on you, this week I thought I'd take a few minutes out to explain the 3.5 types of email addresses

User / Mailbox - This is your personal mailbox. Usually yourname@yourcompany.co.uk.

You normally pay per user mailbox.

Alias / Forwarder - This is simply a re-direct to another email address, it can be of the same domain name (i.e. enquiries@brokenstones.net > sales@brokenstones.net) or can be to a different domain name (i.e. info@busstopgroup.co.uk > contact@brokenstones.net). I use these a lot, either if I want to track where certain enquiries are coming from, or if I think I might want to change which mailbox they get sent to in the future.

One word of warning though, if you've got lots of forwarders it can become difficult to manage.

You do NOT normally have to pay for Aliases.

Group / Shared Mailbox - Sometimes these are the same as a User Mailbox, sometimes they are treated differently, but essentially it's a mailbox that multiple people have access to and you can see when someone else not only read an email in that mailbox, but also if it's been replied to. These are really useful when you've got a team of people who all handle the same emails and you want to know what's been replied to and what's still to deal with...

74

Depending on your email system and provider, sometimes you pay for these sometimes you don't.

Domain Forwarder - (this is the .5) This is more of an advanced topic, but essentially you can **forward all mail** sent to one domain name (like brokenstones.it to another one, like brokenstones.net ... so you send an email to chrisblunt@brokenstones.it and chrisblunt@brokenstones.net existed as a mailbox / alias it would automatically appear in that account.

You do not normally have to pay for Domain forwarders.

Top Tip

As mentioned above, I use Aliases ALOT... two key uses for me are:

To track where specific emails are coming from (either from a sales point of view, or also to see if someone's abusing my email address). This happened a few years ago, suddenly my ebay@brokenstones.net email address started getting a shed load of spam emails, eBay had been hacked and my email address was given away... so all I had to do was change my eBay email to a different address and block the original one...

If I think certain emails will need to go elsewhere in future... this is really useful as you are growing. When I first started out the accounts emails used to come to me, when I got a book keeper I could simply re-point the accounts@ address to her mailbox rather than have to tell everyone to start sending mail over to her instead.

From: Chris Blunt chrisblunt@busstopgroup.co.uk

Sent: 28th August 2014

Subject: **Can I share this with you?**

You've probably seen quite a few emails like this coming through lately, it seems the world and its dog wants to share something with you, and usually you've got no flipping idea who the person is?

Storing and sharing stuff via 'the cloud' has pretty much become 2nd nature now, and the scammers are capitalizing on that, that's why you often end up with an inbox full of stuff that 'looks' like it's from Apple or Google or any of the big names out there... I say 'looks' because it's not actually from them, it's been spoofed (Technical term for impersonating someone else's identity on the internet).

Here's an email I got the other day with someone kindly offering to share their google drive with me...

Tue 12/08/2014 13:49

Bonita Garner , Apps Team <Corine@pgdflexo.com>

Bonita Garner shared Google Drive:0557869 to ▬▬▬@brokenstones.net.

To ◼ Chris Blunt

Accept Bonita Garner Google Drive ID:0557869 request clicking on the link below:

<u>Confirm request</u>

Unfortunately, this email is an automated notification, which is unable to receive replies. We're happy to help you with any questions or concerns you may have. Please contact us directly 24/7 via http://www.google.com/support/

Whatever you do, you need to resist that natural urge to click and find out what they are sharing with you, because it's something rather nasty, and nothing to do with Google Drive...

In fact this particular link actually takes you to someone's website that's been hacked and it'll try to infect your computer with a nasty virus.

Top Tip

Think before you click...

As I've said MANY time before, always hove over the link before your click it, and check it's going to take you where you are expecting...

And if it's not something you are expecting treat it with EXTREME caution...

From: Chris Blunt chrisblunt@busstopgroup.co.uk

Sent: 4th September 2014
Subject: **Apple, Celebs and Naked Pics.**

Now is it just me, but was your first thought when you heard the news about the leaked Naked pics of various celebrities not "oh my god how could apple have let this happen" but more... **"Why on earth have they got naked photos of themselves** on their phone anyway"?

This aside the hacking of a number of celebrity Apple iCloud accounts has made big news this week, and I felt it worth interrupting my normal flow to bring you this important bit of advice to **make sure you're not at the same risk** as they were.

You see the main rumour going round as how their accounts got hacked is down to **passwords**, and the **weakness** of them. Basically there is a little tool which will keep on trying common passwords until it finds one that works (they call it brute force – you **keep on kicking the door till it falls in**).

Here's what you should be doing
The best way to protect yourself in these circumstances is to use a meaningless and cryptic password, and I know not everyone can remember these like I can, so I've put together a handy guide that's been used extensively over the last year or so.

I'm willing to bet at least one of the hacked celebrities was using a password that contained either their name, or the name of one of their family members, perhaps with a date of birth in it too... it's just not good enough these days as an average desktop PC will crack that in a few hours.

Now, do you happen know Jennifer Lawrence's address so I can send her a copy of my book with some tips on Password security? :)

I've said it many times already, and I will keep on mentioning it in the future, but you really, REALLY, should be using good strong passwords.

Giveaway #6 Free Password Guide

Struggling to come up with a decent password you can remember?

Then download my Top Tips for creating secure memorable passwords here:

http://chrisbluntbooks.co.uk/wsh2

From: Chris Blunt chrisblunt@busstopgroup.co.uk

Sent: 11th September 2014
Subject: **Rules is Rules...**

Do you remember when it was exciting to hear that familiar little ping of an e-mail arriving, when it was a novelty to receive a new e-mail, and you'd jump to see who'd just sent you an email?

Doesn't really feel like that anymore does it? Now it's more of an e-mail overload and if you're like me, you dread seeing how many new emails are awaiting your attention in the morning.

I'm currently putting together a guide on effective e-mail management, and I thought I'd share a summary of number 2 on the list with you today (Let me know if you'd like the full guide when it's finished?)

Automatic Rules
You can automatically 'do something' with an email when it arrives, based on the email content. Perhaps there's a specific word or phrase in the subject, it's from a specific person, or you've been cc'd in to the email. You can automatically have outlook move, delete, forward, reply, print, pop up and alert... and a whole load more, all based on what's in the email.

A good example of this is I set any emails received from LinkedIn to go in to a specific LinkedIn folder, they don't clutter up my inbox or distract me, and I can pop in to that folder once or twice a week and scan through what's in there.

Suppose you've got a really important client you need to get back to quickly... You can also get Outlook to pop up a message box to alert you if an e-mail arrives from a specific person.

So how do you use rules in outlook?
The easiest way is to create the rule straight from the e-mail you want to deal with... Simply right click on the email in your inbox, choose Rules >

Create Rule...

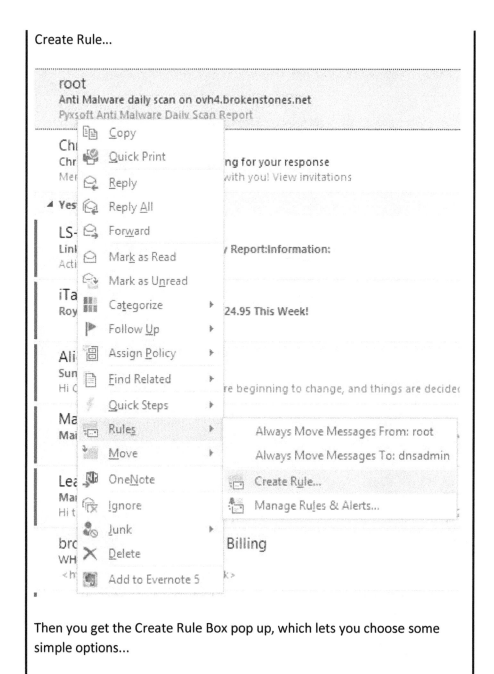

Then you get the Create Rule Box pop up, which lets you choose some simple options...

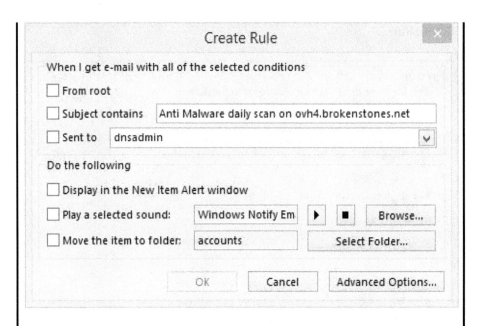

here you can choose to move, play a sound or display an alert based on the Sender (From) the Subject contents or who it's sent too... In my case I want to move this email to a specific folder, but only if it contains specific content in body of the email... So I'm going to set the move item to a folder, but then hit Advanced Options to decide when to move it...

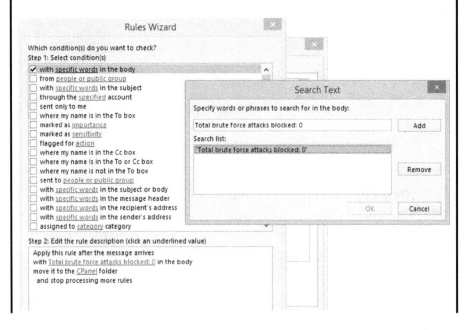

When you hit the advanced options you get the Rules Wizard pop up, you can see in here there are loads of options to choose what to do... I want to move this email if it's got a specific phrase in the body, so I've ticked 'with specific words in the body'.

Hit **next** and choose any extra actions you want to do, I'm also going to mark it as read, then just hit finish.

That's it, your rule is now setup, and next time an email matching your conditions arrives it'll be automatically processed.

I've got rules that...

Move E-Mails sent to a specific address'

Move E-Mails with a specific subject line

Delete emails from a specific company

Set specific emails to automatically delete if I've not actioned them in 1 week

Flag emails sent to a specific address as important

Auto-Forward an email to my accounts department based on the subject.

As I mentioned this is a small extract from the guide I'm creating... I'm also covering a whole load of other useful tips for managing your email, just let me know if you'd be interested in the full guide when it's complete?

Top Tip

I know what it's like to be drowning in e-mail overload, putting in place some small steps to help reduce the amount of emails you have to deal with daily is a real productivity booster...

Think about what emails you get daily / weekly that you pretty much always do the same thing with, can you automate that process so you don't have to manage them?

From: Chris Blunt chrisblunt@busstopgroup.co.uk

Sent: 18th September 2014

Subject: **Are you a One Percenter?**

Speed is of the essence today, we are busy putting together the final preparations for our exhibition stand at the Nation Entrepreneurs conference. We've had to put in a monumental amount of work in a really short space of time, so what better than to share with you **how I get more stuff done than most** on a daily basis... it's all about **the aggregation marginal gains**,

I think it was Sir Clive Woodwood that was quoted as saying *"We didn't improve one thing by 100%, we improved 100 things by 1%"* and that's what I've got for you today, a 1% tip... but don't underestimate its power to make a massive difference to your daily routine.

At a recent I.T. Clinic this is a little tip that got a huge round of "ohhh that's amazing..." and everyone commented on how simple, yet massively useful it was.
This is all about making the things you do most often every day that little bit easier and quicker to do... The truth is this one can really boost your productivity and it's so easy to set-up.

I'm talking about the 'Quick Access Toolbar' in Microsoft Office, it can be found right up at the top left of any Word, Excel, Outlook, PowerPoint (and more) Window...

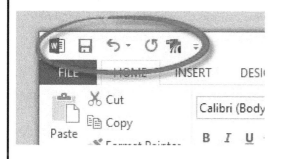

Here you can put almost anything you do regularly in Office so it's just a quick click away, use it for the things you do most often and it will make those tasks even quicker...

I'm often wanting to send my word documents as PDFs to people, so I'd like to pin the 'Send as PDF' option to my Quick Access toolbar... here's how...

Click the little down arrow at the right hand side of the Quick Access Toolbar, You'll either see what you want in the short list (like E-Mail or Quick Print) or click 'More Commands...' if you don't see what you're looking for.

I don't just want to e-mail the document, I want to convert it to a PDF at the same time, so I'm going to click 'More commands...'

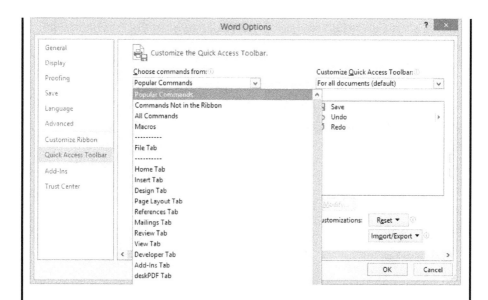

Up pops the more commands box and you'll then see a drop down that currently says 'Popular Commands'. From here you can choose the menu that your chosen command is on, mines on the 'File Tab', so I'm going to select that...

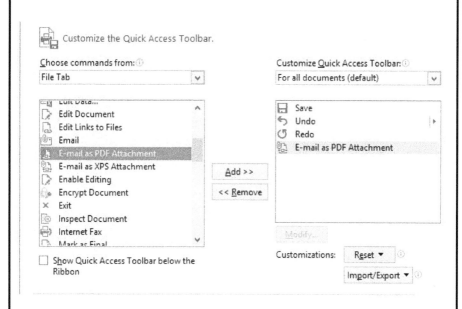

Then you get all the available options on the 'File Tab' in the left hand list, I'm going to scroll down and locate the 'E-mail as PDF Attachment' option, click it, then click Add. You'll notice it then appears in the list window on the left to show you it's been added.

Now just click OK and you'll be back to your document and you'll notice up at the top a new icon has been added, now all you have to do is simply click this and it'll pop straight up with an email window and your document attached as a PDF.

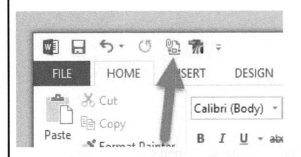

Normally I'd have to make 4 clicks & Mouse Movements - 'File > Share > E-Mail > Send as PDF', now I only have to make one Click! Even if I'm only doing this 4 or 5 times a day it still all adds up over the weeks and months.

The Aggregation of Marginal Gains...

Top Tip

What do you do every day that you could add to the Quick Access Toolbar?

Over the next week be conscious about the things you are doing most often in Word, Excel & Outlook, what would you benefit from popping on the quick access toolbar?

It's these small amount of time saving tricks that add up to a whole heap of extra stuff done every day.

I know I've mentioned this before, but it's still happening, a lot... and it's still a really bad way to do it.

Have you ever wondered why accessing your email seems to go really slow at times?

You see with E-Mail size really does matter, it's definitely not a case of Bigger is Better... and using E-Mail to whiz file attachments all over the place, although may seem easy, it's not a great thing to be doing.

Only last week I was chatting to someone having problems sending an email to a client of theirs, it contained an important document that needed to be there by 5pm... The trouble was the file they were trying to send was 37MB in size and it wasn't going through. Their clients E-Mail system wouldn't allow files over 10MB in size and kept bouncing it back (yes they had sent it 3 times!)

Dispelling the Myth
E-Mail is NOT a File Storage system. The whole way e-mail systems are designed make them bad for storing and transmitting files. I'm not going to go in to the technical mumbo jumbo on why in this email, and I've kind of covered that before (see page 76 of my first book), along with good ways to work around it.

Does it matter that I've got a large mailbox?
In short yes, with all the search that goes on now, your mail client is frequently scanning your emails, and the more that's in there, the longer it takes... this includes file attachments, most modern mail clients will also search the attachments, and generally the larger they are, the longer it takes... so if you've ever wondered why sometimes your email seems REALLY slow, it's probably cause it's doing an index, or searching for something...

Some Practical help

The good news is it's really quite easy to find the large e-mails in your mailbox and do something with them (did you know you can drag emails out of outlook and in to a folder on your computer?)

If you're using Outlook (both on the Mac and on Windows) there is something called 'Search Folders' in here you can tell it to find all files over a certain size so you can do something with them.

Just choose the Folder Tab and New Search folder, and then Scroll down to find 'Large Mail'. (If you're using Outlook 2007 you should have a 'Large Mail' folder already, let me know if you need help!)

Giveaway #7 – Drop Box Free Trial

Drop Box is a great way to store and share information in a safe and secure place, right at your fingertips.

Follow my link to grab yourself a month's trial.

http://chrisbluntbooks.co.uk/wsh2

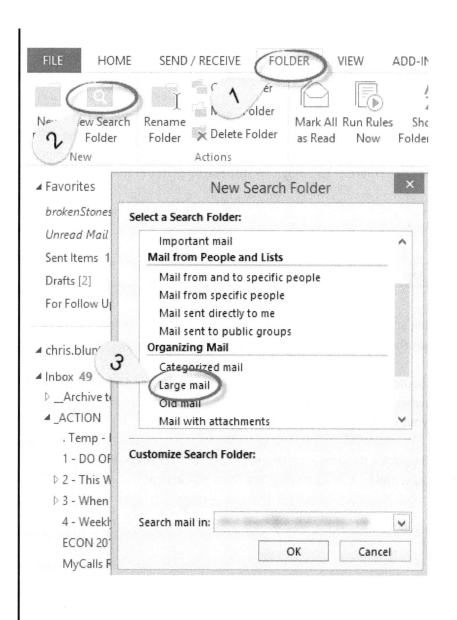

Then you choose the mail size to search for and hit OK. My advice would be to start off with files over 10,000KB (That's 10MB) and clear them out first... then work backwards if you need to.

When you've done that you get a new Search Folder appear at the bottom, when you click in here you'll notice it's started to find some emails, and will take some time to scan everything (depending how much you've got in there!). You might be surprise at what's in there!

Top Tip

Keeping your mailbox free of large file attachments (including photos of the kids the mother-in-law sends you - or is that just me?).

You should regularly scan for large files in your inbox and move them somewhere safe (or delete them if you don't actually need them!). It will help your email run that little bit quicker!

Also if you're a habitual attachment sender, then check out Page 76 of my first book and look at something like Drop-box instead!

From: Chris Blunt chrisblunt@busstopgroup.co.uk

Sent: 2nd October 2014

Subject: **A bit of a character**...

One of the frustrating things about being in I.T. is when you see someone making a right meal of what is really a very simple task. Seriously, it makes my blood boil sometimes and I can't help to butt in and put them straight.

This happened last week, I saw someone trying to create a small document with a few tick boxes on it, to get the tick boxes in the right place they were using a complex system of tables and borders, putting a border round certain cells to form the check-boxes... and they seemed to be struggling somewhat.

The thing is, you can do this ever so easily, with minimal effort, and you don't need to go near tables... It's using something called the 'Character Map', it's a little feature built in to windows and it lets you insert and character from any font you've got installed.

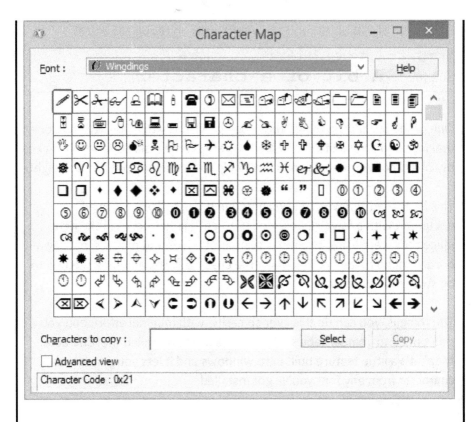

To get a check box simply open up the character map, change to 'windings' font and find the check-box you want...

If you're using Windows 8 simply hit the start button and type 'character' then hit enter and up pop's the character map.

If you're using Windows 7 it's a bit more long winded I'm afraid... Click Start > All Programs > Accessories > System Tools > Character Map.

(If you're on a mac *then in finder you just need to click Edit > Special Characters and you'll get something very similar)*

As you can see there are a whole host of icons to choose from, for check-boxes I tend to use the one 5 rows down on the left... simply double click it then switch back to your word document and hit paste.

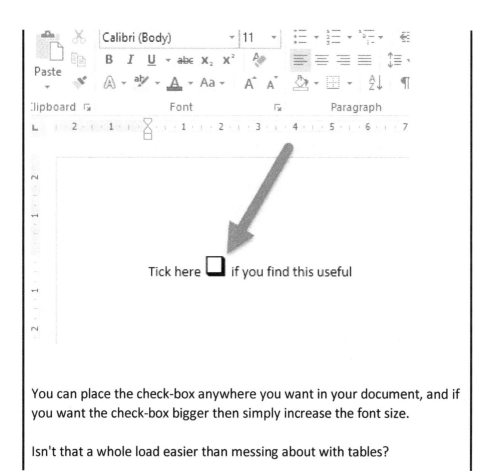

Tick here ☐ if you find this useful

You can place the check-box anywhere you want in your document, and if you want the check-box bigger then simply increase the font size.

Isn't that a whole load easier than messing about with tables?

Top Tip

The Character map is a great, easy way to insert a whole host of symbols or special characters not just check-boxes, explore what's available, whether you need a foreign letter, or perhaps something from the Greek alphabet.

From: Chris Blunt chrisblunt@busstopgroup.co.uk

Sent: 9th October 2014

Subject: Who have you given my email address to?

I'm not being funny, but it doesn't look very professional when someone simply blasts your email address out to all their contacts without asking first.

RANT WARNING!

Yet I see this happening *at-least* on a weekly basis, usually someone I don't know that well has sent an email out to most people in there contact list and just cc'd everyone in... You know the type I'm talking about, there's about 50 people in the 'To' box and you recognize maybe one or two of them...

Would you send a letter out and list the names and addresses of all the people you've just sent it to?

If you're unlucky then you'll get someone on that list that hit's 'Reply All' and sends a really pointless reply and your inbox is bombarded for the next day or two by a whole plethora of replies...

And if you're really unlucky then someone on that e-mail will add you on to their mailing list *"Hey, you obviously know << Test First Name >> so I'm going to send you loads of info about pensions even though I know nothing about you..."*

Now sending out emails is a really easy and convenient way of getting a message out there, and there are a couple of really easy ways you can do that without sharing everyone's e-mail address...

BCC - Stands for Blind Carbon Copy - It'll send someone an e-mail without showing anyone else that you've included that person... have you ever received an email and wondered how it's got to you because you're not in the address list? Chances are you've been Bcc'd. This is usually used by popping yourself in the top box, and all your recipients in the BCC Box... (You might also need to click 'show BCC' in your mail client)

E-Mail Marketing List - Really if you're sending out anything that's vaguely business / sales / marketing related you should be using an e-mail marketing service... most are dead easy to use and usually free to get started with... MailChimp is a good service (and free for up to 1,000 people on your list) - I'm not going to go in to the detail of it today, but if you do want to know more just drop me an email back and I'll send you some more info over.

Top Tip

Copying all your contacts in to a single e-mail does not look very professional, some people are very protective over their e-mail address and may take great offence.

At the very least you should be blind copying people in (BCC), but if it's something you send out regularly then look at using an e-mail marketing service.

I've seen a whole variety of ways other people have tried to solve this particular issue, but it's actually really, really simple...

I've seen people change the font size to make word documents easier to read, I've even seen people lower their screen resolution so stuff appears bigger on their monitor, when all they are trying to do is just make something easier to read on the screen...

All they need to do in most situations is zoom in or out, and I've got a really quick easy way to do this in most of the programs you'll use day to day.

You'll notice, especially in Chrome or IE, that the zoom in/out buttons are hidden... but that's OK cause the easiest way to zoom is to use the mouse wheel...

It's really easy, and another little time saver, all you've got to do is hold down the CTRL key that's on the left and right of your keyboard (either one will do).

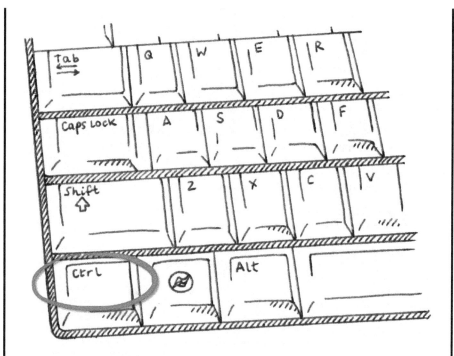

You can then you the Mouse Scroll wheel to scroll up or down to zoom in or out... try it now...

I find it especially useful when I'm reading a PDF, often text can be quite small and being able to scroll in or out really quickly is really handy...

HINT: If you're a Mac User and find it doesn't work, just open up your system preferences and search for 'Zoom' there's an option to turn it on & off.

Top Tip

Another devastating simple time saving tip...

Use the CTRL + Mouse Wheel to zoom in and out... just hold down the CTRL Key (usually on the left and right of your keyboard - you can use either one... I usually find the left one easiest myself). Just hold down the CTRL key and use the Mouse Scroll wheel when you're in Word, Excel, Internet Explorer, Chrome, PDF Reader... in fact lots of programs let you do this... just try it.

Do you remember this?

5 years ago this was the major phone, there was no such thing as an iPad and we were still watching Analogue TV!

It's fair to say quite a lot has changed in the world of technology in 5 years, yet I'm still meeting people on a regular basis who have computers older than this and haven't realised just how much has changed...

The trouble is the pace of technology moves so quickly, that it's easy for your computer to quickly become outdated.

So how long should your computer last?
Well that depends... it depends what your using it for, and what you get in

the first place. I know it sounds a bit of a cop out, but there is no hard and fast one rule fits all answer.

If you think about the upheaval of changing computers, moving all your data across, getting your e-mail re-setup, installing all the variety of programs you use (and finding the license keys!) then it's not something you really want to be doing every 6 months!

I usually advice most of my clients to **plan on a 3-5 year life-cycle**, depending on what they use their computers for and what they get in the first place. Oh and you want to make sure you get a manufacturer backed warranty to cover you for the entire life-cycle of the computer.

If you're using a computer that's more than 5 years old you should definitely think about upgrading it... especially if it's running Windows XP or Windows Vista (its well over 5 years if you're using either of those operating systems!)

Top Tip

Generally you should be planning for a 3 Year lifespan for your computers, think about that when choosing a new computer and looking at what you pay for it. It can often be a big upheaval changing to a new computer and you don't want to be going through that too often.

Oh and always make sure you get a 3 year **onsite** manufacturer warranty, it'll cover you if anything does go wrong, and the last thing you want to be doing is send it off for a week or so whilst it gets fixed!

From: Chris Blunt chrisblunt@busstopgroup.co.uk

Sent: 30th October 2014

Subject: **Why MAC is better than PC**

Wherever you go, you'll always find an Apple fan raving how much better the Mac is to the windows PC, and d'you know what, they are partly right...

I'm probably going to upset a few people now...

You see yes, if you are comparing a nice shiny Mac Book Pro to a £300 Laptop from PC World then yes it is much better... but you're not comparing like for like.

A mid-range Mac book Pro costs about £1,200, spend that on a windows laptop and you'll also get a pretty good computer that will be a good match for a Mac Book.

You see Apple don't make a bad computer, but there are plenty of sub £500 windows computers available, and you just can't compare them.

Then there is using it...
Now if you're not used to using a Mac, you'll also find it a big change navigating you way around (yes even more than the hysteria that was made about the windows 8 start menu).

It's something mac worshippers omit to mention when encouraging people to switch. I've had to sit with a number of people that have plumped for a Mac on the belief it would change their lives for the better, but instead they've had a big learning curve getting used to a completely different environment and way of working.

And another thing...
Another beef I have with switching over to Mac is not stopping to consider what you actually use your computer for day to day... if you are predominantly Cloud based then it's not so much of an issue, but if you've

got software that needs to run on windows then it's not such a smart idea moving to a mac...

And finally...
It's probably a good thing I'm out of the country at the moment, otherwise I'd likely get lynched, but in all seriousness **it's not a case of Mac is Better than Windows,** or vice versa, as with all I.T. it's **whatever fits your circumstances best**...

I'm not some big Mac hater, I just believe in **making sure you've got the right equipment** for you, for some people that will be a Mac, but for a lot of others if you're thinking of spending that kind of money you'll be best off investing it in a decent windows computer.

I've actually got a Mac at home, my eldest daughter loves it, we use it for browsing the web, the occasional bit of work and talking with the extended family (via Skype & Face-time), it does exactly what we need it to.

Top Tip

If you are feeling swayed by the argument to get an Apple Mac, then first stop to consider what kind of windows computer you can get for the same money. Then look at all the things you use your computer for day to day, does anything there rely on using Windows?

Finally are you happy to adjust to a new user interface, and prepared to go through a bit of a learning curve.

I'm not trying to scare you off, I just want to make sure you understand everything involved, remember the phrase "the grass is always greener on the other side".

From: Chris Blunt chrisblunt@busstopgroup.co.uk

Sent: 6th November 2014

Subject: **I didn't send that e-mail**

Have you also been getting a load of 'Undeliverable Mail' messages from people you've never heard of?

We've had a lot of people get in touch lately because they have been getting 'Undeliverable' Messages to e-mails that they've not even sent... you know the message you get that says "I'm sorry this email could not be delivered to this address"...

They are worried someone's been accessing their e-mail account and sending out loads of e-mails to a load of random people...

The thing is it's usually got nothing to do with your e-mail account, someone's just 'spoofing' you're e-mail address... and you are getting what's known as 'backscatter'... How dare they I hear you say, they can't possibly do that...

But think about it, how easy is it for you to write a letter claiming it to be from someone else, all you've got to do is write the 'Reply To' Address on the envelope as something other than your own... and that's exactly the same as how e-mail works, you can easily change the from or reply to address on an e-mail, and that's what's happening in most of these cases.

So what can you do about it?

The short answer is not a lot... it's somewhat outside of your control, it's a 3rd party sending an email to another 3rd party, it's not actually got very much to do with you, other than they are using your email address.

There are a few things you can do to help reduce how much 'backscatter' you get...

The first is checking where your e-mail address is published... ideally you want to find NO Results when you search your e-mail address on Google...

The more places it's published on the internet, the more likely it is to be picked up by spammers and spoofed.

Secondly make sure you've got your domain name and e-mail set-up properly to take advantage of anti-spam measures like SPF and DKIM (I'm not going to go in to what they are here, just ask your I.T. guy if you're not sure).

Finally, make sure you're using a decent anti-spam filter, which will help reduce the amount of undeliverable emails you get back (it can't block them all, as some may be legitimate from e-mails that you've sent yourself...)

Top Tip

E-Mail Spoofing and Backscatter can cause a drastic increase in the amount of unwanted mail that you get.

To help reduce this check if your email address is published anywhere on the web https://www.google.co.uk/webhp?q="<< Your Email Address >>" (Just pop your email address in to Google with Double Quotes around it).

Then anywhere you find your e-mail address work to get it removed... - for public listings I usually use a different e-mail address that's re-directed to my main address - that way I can change or remove it if I need to quite easily..

Give away #8 – Free Email Address Check

Check to make sure your e-mail address is not being exposed anywhere on the web.

http://chrisbluntbooks.co.uk/wsh2

From: Chris Blunt chrisblunt@busstopgroup.co.uk

Sent: 13th November 2014

Subject: **Over your limit**

I've had a few people flag this up to me in the last couple of weeks, and as it's been a little while since I've touched on this subject I figured it was worth bringing it up again.

You may have seen an email a little bit like this come through, letting you know you are over your mailbox size limit...

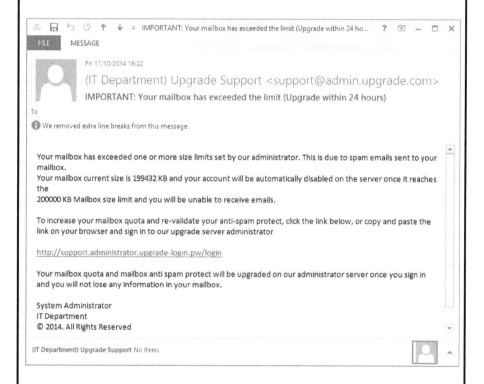

Now if you're someone who keeps a lot of email in your inbox (and I know a few people like that!) then you may have received similar messages to this in the past, and that's what the people who have sent this particular e-mail are hoping...

You see it's actually a scam e-mail (the technical term for this particular email is a 'phishing email' – In the interests of public information, I've clicked through to this particular site from a 'safe' machine... I STRONGLY recommend you do NOT click that link.

When you click through you get to a page that looks like this...

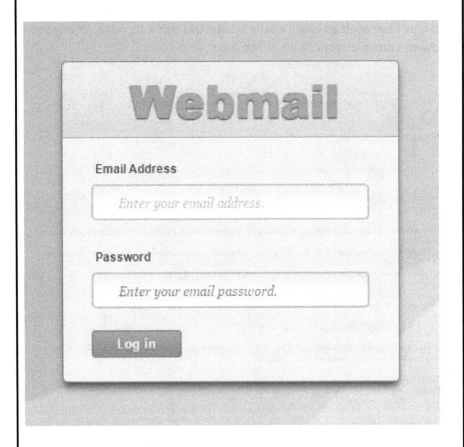

If you're on one of standard cPanel Mail platforms you'll be familiar with that login page, and that's exactly what they are hoping, so you just pop your email address and password in as normal, which when you do that, it then pauses for a few moments (like it's trying to login), then it comes up with a message saying 'Upgraded Successfully' (That's the clever bit…), cause then you think nothing of it, that it's all worked OK and you'll go about your normal day.

Now the scammers have got your E-Mail address and E-Mail password, they can really easily login to your email account and start making your life hell.

Don't do it! – But what if you already have?

And if you have recently had an email like this and clicked the link then you need to go change your e-mail password right now! Then check your deleted items, and then go change your passwords across every other website you login to.

Why check your deleted items?

A common trick now is to gain access to your e-mail, then go do a password reset on your Facebook, eBay and amazon accounts (and any other account they can find), then they'll delete the password reset e-mails so you don't know about it… ouch!

Top Tip

When you get any E-mail asking you to login to your e-mail treat it with extreme caution… Your email account is pretty much the key to your life these days.

If you at all unsure about whether something is legitimate or not, assume it isn't and do some more research to prove otherwise.

From: Chris Blunt chrisblunt@busstopgroup.co.uk

Sent: 20th November 2014

Subject: **It needs to be upgraded**

You know, it never ceases to amaze me how much effort is put in to some areas of these things, yet such big gaping holes are left elsewhere.

Tracey sent this in to me on Sunday evening, it's a new one that I've not seen before, I have to say the language makes me chuckle a little bit "You need to upgrade your MICROSOFT", but if you're in a rush and you just skim the email for an overview you can see how it would be easy to click the Upgrade button.

So here it is, officially from me, it's a fake e-mail (There's a few other clues too! I've listed them below).

This is what it looks like...

From: ebay@ebay.co.uk
Subject: Urgent Message - You need to upgrade your account now !!
Date: Sun, 16 Nov 2014 19:34:01 +0100

To make sure emails from MICROSOFT Mail go into your inbox and not the junk folder, add suppport@microsoft.co.uk to your address book.

Your Classic version of MICROSOFT is closing. You need to upgrade now

Hello,

The Classic version of MICROSOFT will be replaced by our new version on 19th NOV 2014. So it's time to upgrade, before you lose your email access.

When you upgrade your MICROSOFT

Your email service won't be affected and you'll keep all your old contacts, folders and messages. Plus you'll get:

- faster email
- the latest spam protection
- unlimited email storage.

How you can upgrade your account

Click on the link below and follow the instructions. You'll also need to agree to some new terms and conditions. CLICK HERE TO UPGRADE YOUR ACCOUNT

Thanks for choosing MICROSOFT,

Satya Nadella
Microsoft Corporation, CEO

They are likely playing on the fact you may have heard of the recent changes to the Office 365 program, but if you've been paying attention to my previous e-mails and stopped to hover over the Upgrade Link before you click, you'll spot something's not quite right...

ı storage.

ıe your account

ı and follow the instructi
conditions. CLICK HERE TO UPGRADE YOUR ACCOUNT

http://micropix.net/includes/conf.html
Click to follow link

SOFT

Oh, and finally if you've not picked up from the e-mail content, or from the actual link the email is a scam, then just check out who it says it's from...

Why would you get an email from eBay telling you your Microsoft Account needs to be upgraded?

Well done Tracey for the Spot and thanks for bringing it to my attention, I've popped a little something in the post for you.

Top Tip

I know I keep repeating it a lot, but this stuff really does save you a whole heap of trouble...

Always Hover over E-Mail Links BEFORE you click them. I'm sure I could come up with some Green Cross Code style motto...

STOP - HOVER - THINK.... what do you think?

And if you are ever unsure about anything then just ask us!

From: Chris Blunt chrisblunt@busstopgroup.co.uk

Sent: 27th November 2014
Subject: **Shouldn't you be keeping this private?**

There's been a lot of focus put on security this last year, there's been a few high profile issues (do you remember the heart-bleed thing? Or when eBay managed to expose 145 Million account details back in may?)

To combat this we've seen a big push to increase awareness along with the security of the software and systems you are using every day.

One such 'improvement' is the way Google Chrome deals with websites that don't have a valid Security Certificate...

You've probably been presented with this screen the last few months, we've certainly been getting a lot more calls from our clients unsure what to do...

Your connection is not private

Attackers might be trying to steal your information from **brokenstones.net** (for example, passwords, messages or credit cards).

Advanced   Back to safety

The good thing about what they've done here is it makes a log of people stop and think (Certainly first time I saw it, I stopped for a short while to check it out in more detail...

But, judging by the number of calls we get about this now, it's not very easy to work out how to continue through if you're sure you're at the right place...

It's good because you really should be taking note of these messages, and not just blindly clicking through (I know I'm guilty of that sometimes!!), but it does feel like they've gone a bit too far with it!

So if you're still struggling, here's how to confirm you know this is a safe site...

Your connection is not private

Attackers might be trying to steal your information from **brokenstones.net** (for example, passwords, messages or credit cards).

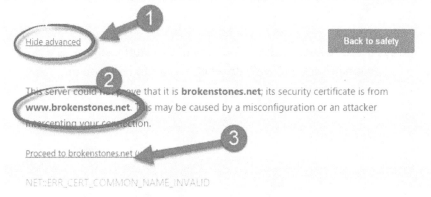

Hide advanced

Back to safety

This server could not prove that it is **brokenstones.net**; its security certificate is from **www.brokenstones.net**. This may be caused by a misconfiguration or an attacker intercepting your connection.

Proceed to brokenstones.net (

NET::ERR_CERT_COMMON_NAME_INVALID

1. First you need to click the 'Advanced' Link - That gives us some more options...

2. Now read the message carefully... In my case it's telling me the website is actually identifying itself as '**www.**brokenstones.net' whereas I only typed in 'brokenstones.net' - I pretty sure that's OK and I'm safe to continue through. - Another common message you'll see here is 'Certificate Expired' which means the site owners not renewed their Security certificate... it's usually worth you double checking with them if it's something important you're doing!

3. Once you're happy it's safe to carry on to the website, click the 'Proceed to <website>' link and then you'll see the site as normal.

Top Tip

Whenever you are entering sensitive information (like a username and password and ESPECIALLY credit card details!!) make sure the webpage you are using is using a proper security certificate... you'll be able to tell this by a green bar or tick at the top of your web browser...

As always if you're ever unsure about any of this stuff just give us a call or drop me an email back and we'll do what we can to help you out.

From: Chris Blunt chrisblunt@busstopgroup.co.uk

Sent: 4th December 2014
Subject: **The rudest e-mail I've ever written**

It used to be floppy, then it got hard, and now someone else is holding it for you... However, that brings all sorts of issues with it, and if you're not careful you can end up in a lot of trouble and even in breach of several laws...

Before you thinking I've gone completely mad, you should understand in the last few years there have been massive leaps forward in cloud storage (AKA storing your data somewhere on the internet for easy and convenient access).

The trouble is here in the UK there are some strict rules and regulations about what we can store, and where. You'll be glad to know I'm not going to go in to a full spiel on the data protection act, you can easily google that, and whilst your there look up 'Sending personal data overseas' too... (BTW, as a business owner, or someone responsible for information security in your business you really should be aware of it too!)

What I've got for you today is a couple of solutions to that problem, you see most people I talk to don't have a clue where there data is stored or how it's protected. When you are storing or backing up your data remotely you really need to make sure it's secure (In truth, even if you are storing it locally you need to make sure it's secure!!).

I'm regularly asked about trustworthy cloud backup services, (Including Donna who posed the question via our Facebook page last week – *thanks Donna!*). I've even had to get detailed information to satisfy the FCA for one of the services we recommended.

We've got two types of backup services available at the moment, both are £1.25 per Gigabyte of data.

We've also got a 3rd, brand new, fixed price, unlimited storage service launching in January, if you're interested in either of these services just visit http://brokenstones.co.uk/contact-us/get-quote/ and we'll be in touch with more info.

Top Tip

Three things you should be looking at for any cloud data service you are using are:

Where is the data stored? (Preferably here in the UK!)

How is the data encrypted? (Who is able to decrypt it? Ideally you want to encrypt it before it leaves your computer!)

What kind of Service Level Agreement do they offer (What happens if they have a problem?)

Pricewise services vary vastly, but there is often a reason for this, check exactly what you are getting for your money.

Give away #9 – 2 Months Free Backup Service

Hop on over to my link and grab yourself 2 free months of our business grade backup service, make sure everything important is always backed up just in case!

http://chrisbluntbooks.co.uk/wsh2

From: Chris Blunt chrisblunt@busstopgroup.co.uk

Sent: 12th December 2014

Subject: **Going off on a bit of a tangent**

You might think this a little bit odd, but over the last few years there has been one topic I've not really covered, to me it's been kind of obvious, and to help me explain I've got a little story about my bathroom... bear with me if this starts to get a little weird...

I've been having my bathroom done, it's the only one in our house at the moment, so it's been a bit of an upheaval, now aside from the electrics I could have done the rest of the work myself if I'd wanted too, I'm sure it would have been fun to get the hammer drill out and rip down all the tiles and plaster, google is littered with videos on how to plaster your walls, and how hard can tiling be anyway??

But I also know that if I had chosen to do it all myself it would have taken considerably longer than the 3 weeks it's taken so far (we move back in this evening!!), you probably would have stubbed your toe on a floor tile that I'd not got quite level... water would have seeped through the side of the bath where I'd not sealed it properly, and in a year or so stuff would start falling off the wall.

You see, I'm not a bathroom fitter, I'm not a plasterer, I'm not a tiller, there are people out there who do are experts at that, they know if a box of my tiles is slightly warped and to use them on the window reveals and edges so you don't notice, they know the best Radiator valves to get so you don't bash your ankles when you're half asleep in the morning, they know how to do it properly so my bathrooms going to last another 30 years (yes the old one did have BROWN tiles - check out the picture!)

OK, before you think I've gone completely loopy, I probably need to bring this back on track... you see I come across people every day that have tried to manage their I.T. on their own, or maybe got the 17 year old office apprentice to do it – because all the youths of today know computers right?

But then they come to me because something's gone wrong... maybe their lucky and it's just cause they keep 'stubbing their toe on something' – like their e-mail keeps going missing, but often it's because the bath's just dropped through the floor boards because water was leaking and no-one noticed till it was too late – i.e. they've just been hacked and had £30,000 stolen from their bank account because they didn't have the right security in place (I've actually seen two separate people who have had this exact thing happen to them... but that's another story...)

If you've been following my emails over the last two years you'll know these are all about delivering good, valuable advice, and this is a rare occasion, it's just I believe so strongly in this, that we add so much value it'd be doing a dis-service if I didn't bring this up now...

I can really help you with this, I.T. Support & Advice is the core of my business, I'd like to think we are one of the best in the country at this (and I've got a good amount of evidence to support that!).

Alternatively if it's just you, or maybe one other person than you'll fit right in to our I.T. club – I've put together a special offer for you right here: http://mbitclub.co.uk/toptips2014/

Please don't let my unashamed plug above detract from this message, I want you to know that this is probably the single most important piece of advice I can give you, employing the services of a good I.T. Company is invaluable. The good ones of us out there (see below for how to spot us!) will save you time, money and whole host of problems.

If you've already got one, great, but if not then go and find one, we are worth it.

Top Tip

Now I know I've gone off on a [very] weird tangent here, but this is probably the single biggest most important thing you should know... don't try and do I.T. yourself, as I.T. professionals we spend all day, every day living and breathing I.T.

There's a couple of things you should look out for with your I.T. support provider:

Make sure they are **CompTIA Accredit UK Trustmark+ certified** – it's the best quality standard available in our industry. We're audited every year, and you should find an entry on the Trustmark directory like ours here: BS Net Trustmark

What other certifications do they have? Look for some of the Major Brands, like Microsoft Cisco, Draytek... And look for more than just 'registered' or 'Authorized' for example Microsoft have 'Silver' and 'Gold' partner levels which you have to go through a certification process for. (Usually exams and references from clients)

Anyone can call themselves an 'I.T. expert', but these 'badges' show we've invested in our business and basically show we know what we're on about.

Give away #10 – Helpdesk Packages

If you are office based with a number of staff, then you'll want to talk to me about our Helpdesk Packages just visit:

http://chrisbluntbooks.co.uk/wsh2

Rachael will schedule a call for us – no pressure, let's just chat.

From: Chris Blunt chrisblunt@busstopgroup.co.uk

Sent: 18th December 2014

Subject: **Top Tips**

I don't want to seem like a bit of a heartless monster, but we had to have a little chuckle in the office this last week.

Now we don't usually laugh at our customer's expense, but in this case, you just couldn't help it.

You see we had a phone call from someone we'd just supplied and installed a new PC in to, it'd been in 3-4 weeks and they called us up to say it wasn't working, wouldn't even turn on… which was odd, because we could see it OK in our monitoring dashboard.

I'll spare you the long story of diagnosis, but it turned out to be the monitor that looked to be broken.

Now this particular customer is only just down the road from us, so one of the guys decided just to pop out with a spare monitor and go and have a look… and that's when it all became obvious… and what made us all chuckle more than Brian's Christmas jumper…

Now we have seen this once or twice before, but it's usually the cleaners or some other 3rd party, not the actual individual themselves.

On the desk was a lovely festively decorated monitor, complete with flashing lights, however, to connect the lights they'd diligently traced the power cable from the PC back to the wall, and seeing the other plug next to it, assuming it was unused unplugged it to plug their lights in!

Now clearly it's be a pretty lame e-mail if all I had for you was "Don't unplug your monitor" – although you would be surprised how often we do see things like that happen (usually the cleaners, or the PAT tester guy, we've even had someone take down part of a network so they could straighten their hair!)

Most people are aware they should have some kind of power protection for their servers, phone system and network – but did you know you can also get some inexpensive protection for your desktop too, which in this case would have started beeping frantically, and at the very least caused the individual to pick up the phone and call us, if not to plug the thing back in!

Top Tip

Believe it or not, there is actually a way to know if you've done something daft like unplug the power to your computer... and that's to get yourself a 'UPS' – Uninterruptable Power Supply – more commonly they ensure you're computer doesn't just go off during a power cut, and gets a nice stable power feed without the ever increasing power spikes and brown outs...

Getting a small Desktop UPS is a great addition to your computer setup. It provides a short period of battery power to keep your computer running in the event of a power cut, as a minimum enough time for your computer to shut itself down safely, without losing any work, and for most short power outages will keep you working throughout. They also provide a handy 'beeping' sound alerting you in case someone's unplugged or even turned the power off accidentally...

You can pick up a good quality unit for around £80, and if you've spent money on a decent PC or Mac, why would you risk that for the sake of £80? We use them on every desktop here.

From: Chris Blunt chrisblunt@busstopgroup.co.uk

Sent: 8th January 2015

Subject: **Making a fresh start...**

If you're like me you'll have come back from Festive break itching to get going with loads of new ideas and anything that holds you back, even just for a few moments, will really get your goat...

So here's a little New Year tip from me to give you a little boost...

You see, whether you use a Mac, a Windows PC or something completely different, they could all use the same thing from time to time... and that's a fresh start.

I'm talking specifically about a 'proper' restart or shutdown... you see there is a difference between just closing the lid or putting your computer to sleep and actually turning it off properly...

Most laptops and desktops are setup now so that when you close the lid or click the power button they just go to sleep... then save what you're doing, so that when you press the on button again they fire up quicker and you're back up and running that bit quicker...

But every once in a while it pays to do a proper reboot or switch off. The start of the New Year seems like the ideal time for that doesn't it?

I'll spare you the technical gumpf, but it gives all sorts of systems and programs a bit of a clean, and you'll find things run a little bit quicker than they did before...

I find the same applies with my iPad and iPhone too, every once in a while I turn them off and back on again, it just clears stuff out...

So before you call it a day this evening choose 'Shutdown' or at the very least 'Reboot', and wish you a happy new year ;) (Or maybe that's just me!!)

Top Tip

Shutting the Lid or pressing sleep is NOT the same as rebooting or shutting down.

Giving your computer a Reboot everyone once in a while is a good thing to do... If you can't afford the time it takes, then set it going whilst you nip out for lunch, or know you'll be away for 20 minutes or so...

Same goes for your phone and tablet's giving them a restart once in a while is a good thing to do...

On June the 30th this year we are getting an extra second added to the day... we'll forget that, how would you like a whole extra day?

Cause that's the basis for this week's Top Tip, I've got a really quick, easy, time saving tip that will give you at least 1 extra day per year. It's something pretty much everyone I meet can make use of, and once you master it it'll be one of those things you just do without thinking...

If you think about it, a lot of your time on the computer these days is spent switching between different things... I'm usually alternating between writing I.T. plans in Word, referencing technical details on the web, or a PDF Spec Sheet and jumping in and out of our quoting system.

I'll cut the waffle now... using the mouse to switch between things the whole time is slow, so any way you can reduce the time it takes to switch is good news... and the good news hear is it's dead, dead easy, and once you get the hang of it it's just like walking up to the curb stone, you do it without thinking...

When you've got more than one thing open just hold down the ALT key and press TAB (The key above caps lock)... you'll get a little window pop up like this... (On the Mac it's COMMAND + TAB)

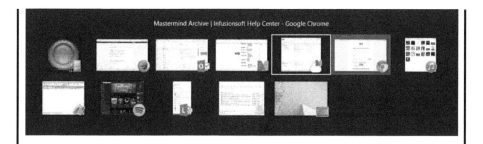

Then if you keep ALT held down and keep on pressing tab, it'll cycle along the open programs... find the one you want and let go of ALT... you'll notice you are now using the program you've just selected...

The REALLY neat bit now (and super, super useful when you're using word + another program...) is if you just press ALT + TAB quickly now, you're back to your original program... try that a few times now... just press ALT + TAB quickly a few times and notice how you switch back and forth between the two programs... Can you see just how much quicker that is than picking up the mouse and going hunting for it along the taskbar?

Top Tip

Here's the interesting bit...

If you only switched between programs 24 times in a day... then in year you've just found yourself a whole extra day!! And that's assuming you're pretty quick with the mouse and change programs in under 6 seconds... One whole extra day... is that worth spending 20 minutes learning and practicing this technique for?

Hold down ALT, then Press TAB (The key above caps lock) (COMMAND + TAB on the MAC)

From: Chris Blunt chrisblunt@busstopgroup.co.uk

Sent: 22nd January 2015

Subject: **This response shocked me**

It may come as no surprise to you that I sent an email last week... but what surprised me was the response I got back...

I actually had this twice since the New Year, but last weeks left me flabbergasted...
I'd met someone at a networking meeting that day and I had a bit of potential business to introduce to them, so I picked up their business card and sent an email over to the address on the card.

The response I got back was "This e-mail address does not exist"... (This didn't surprise me too much, this happens more often than you'd think...) so I picked up the phone and gave her a quick call... that's where my surprise came...

She told me her I.T. people had recently changed her email address, and promptly gave me her new one...

This left me quite shocked and feeling somewhat angry, not at the lady herself, but at her IT people, you see changing your email address is not a big issue, but losing one you've been using for years is...

And in most circumstances it's really easy to avoid that. On almost every email platform you can setup what's known as an 'Alias' this is a simple forward to your new e-mail address, so all e-mails to your old address arrive in your new inbox.

Anyway I'm pleased to say after a brief conversation, I was able to tell her exactly what she needed to ask her I.T. people to do, they did, and now her old e-mail address gets through to her too... now she's just left wondering how many emails she's actually missed in the last two months... (And I'm pleased to say is switching all her I.T. over to us!)

Top Tip

Daft as it sounds, check the e-mail address on your business card. We're only 3 weeks in to 2015 and I've already met two people who have an email address that DOES NOT WORK on their business card!

Setting up an e-mail alias is dead easy and is almost always free, an alias simply forwards email to one or more e-mail addresses on the same domain name (i.e. sales@mydomain.com to name@mydomain.com).

You can usually also setup a 'forward' which will forward an email address to an external email account – just be a bit careful with this, if you're forwarding a lot of email you sometimes find your forwarded e-mail ends up I the spam folder. (It's always best to ask!). We do this a lot when we're moving people from their btconnect.com email account to their own domain name so you don't have to keep logging in to two email accounts.

From: Chris Blunt chrisblunt@busstopgroup.co.uk

Sent: 29th January 2015

Subject: **Is your system down?**

I know you're probably going to think this is a really weird subject for me to bring up, but perhaps it might just make you think a little differently...

You may have heard, two weeks ago Lichfield had another Power Cut, it was around 4pm and being winter it had already got dark, as the alarms started to sound I raced through to the I.T. Office to find my team had already started our DR procedures. Brian was shutting down all but our critical systems to preserve the remaining battery backup power and the others were on the phones contacting our local clients to check if they needed any help.

You see this wasn't the first time this had happened, and my team knew from last time what needed to be done. Along with all the other businesses in our road, we'd had a power cut 18 months ago.

Here's the bit I don't really get... you see just like last time, within a few minutes there was a flurry of people rushing out of all the other buildings, jumping in their cars and going home... all except us, the I.T. guys...

You see we seem to be conditioned that we need our computers to do any work. But in 99% of cases, that's not strictly true.

Certainly as an I.T. company ourselves there is lots, and I mean LOTS we can do without a computer at all. Does that sound a bit weird? I know it's hard to imagine now, but we didn't always have computers in our offices, and yes our working practices may have changed a bit, but it doesn't mean we have to just give up and go home if we can't use our computers.

You see computers are there to help us do our job, not replace what we used to do. Think about it, does your business really need to just stop if you lose power? There are loads of things that can be done (Certainly my team got immense benefit from an impromptu training session and team bonding).

If all else fails, how about a bit of Staff Training, pick an element of your business and discuss how you could improve it... or if it's just you then how a bit of business planning & development.

At the very least make a list of the things you need on your computer for next time you're without it.

So what would you do if you had a power cut today? How much would it affect your business? Could you keep on working? Or would you simply go home?

Top Tip

Remember, your business does not have to simply stop when the power goes off. Just cause your system is down, doesn't mean you can't do any work!

Having a plan for what to do in a power cut is a great idea, it does not have to be wasted time, do that job you've been putting off for ages, or deliver a staff training piece on a new service, product or way of working.

Also make sure you've got relevant contact details for who you'd need to call (like your web guy to pop a message on your website?)

From: Chris Blunt chrisblunt@busstopgroup.co.uk

Sent: 5th February 2015

Subject: **Someone really should know better!**

Some people really should know better when it comes to computers... anyone who works for me for instance, that's why I'm singling out a member of my staff this week, but it did make me think, if it was a problem for them, then who else is it affecting?

Their problem was simple, outlook kept on asking for their e-mail password every time they started it up... every time... it's not the first time I've seen this either, it seems to be quite a common complaint... you'll have probably seen this box before?

Odd thing is, there's a really simple fix... the trouble is some people are in such a rush they look straight over it. (As was the case for my member of staff...)

Yep you guessed it, you just need to tick the 'Remember my Password' box... it's THAT simple, yet it's probably one of the most common password related issues we get...

It's not just passwords where this applies though, there's all manner of 'issues' we see that are fixed simply by reading the message and/or ticking the right box...

Why? Because we seemed conditioned to just click 'OK' or 'next' without actually reading what we've been asked... I know I do it myself, I hit next and then think "What did that box just say?"

Top Tip

As daft as it sounds, simply pausing and actually reading what your computer is asking you is not a bad idea... Generally speaking the messages are quite straight forward and helpful, and if you don't understand what they are asking then you only need to ask!

You know that message that keeps popping up that you keep on meaning to pass on, but the thought of typing it out is just not worth it, or maybe you just write down the bit you think is important?

We see it a lot on the helpdesk, a customer will often email, or even phone up trying to read out the message that's on the screen, and often it's full of mumbo jumbo that just doesn't make sense... I've even had someone print out a page, scan it back in, then e-mail it across...

Well there is an easier way... a really easy way to capture the message and send it over without having to write is out or try to pronounce cryptic words... there's a really quick keyboard shortcut to take a quick photo of it and then email over... I use it loads, and it's dead easy for you to use too...

On a Windows PC Just Hit 'ALT + PRINT SCREEN' – this takes an instant screenshot of the currently active window, then just open up an email and press CTRL + V to paste it in there... (Or if that's not working for you paste it in to Word...)

If you're on a Mac it's slightly different... you need to press COMMAND + SHIFT + 4, then Press the Spacebar, then choose the window you want to capture. You'll then get an image saved to your desktop for you to do with what you want...

I use this for all sorts of stuff... not just sending error messages! For instance if there's something wrong with my website I want to email my web guy about, pull it up in the browser window then take a screenshot of the whole window and send it over... it saves having to describe how and where you see the problem.

There's loads of other applications for this too... It's not just for reporting error messages... It's also useful if you've submitted something important and want to capture the confirmation page, or the reference number. Also if you're creating user guides or training manuals... As I mentioned above, it can also come in really handy when working with a 3rd party, sending a quick screenshot can but much, much easier than trying to explain something verbally...

If you're doing a lot of screenshots there is a really nifty piece of software I use called **SnagIt**... it makes taking screenshots even easier, and lets you annotate them too... Its £30 and you can visit:

www.chrisbluntbooks.co.uk/wsh2 if you're interested...

From: Chris Blunt chrisblunt@busstopgroup.co.uk

Sent: 19th February 2015

Subject: **So where did you stick it?**

This popped up earlier this week and I thought you'd find it useful, it was one of those *"ahh, I wish you'd told me that before"* type moments... I'd hate to think how much time has been wasted by missing out on this...

Have you ever wondered when you download something in your web browser where it goes to?

If you're like me, most of the time you open the file straight up and then it's done with... but sometimes you start downloading something, then get distracted and it vanishes... what a lot of people do next is just go download it again... or sometimes they go hunting for their 'Downloads folder', try to remember what it was called and find it in there...

But there's another way, a quick simple way to see your latest downloads...

Just Hit CTRL + J and up pops your latest downloads, all in date order... so your latest download is right at the top...

(Or on Safari for the Mac use COMMAND + OPTION + L)

I'll be honest with you, I use CTRL + J a LOT! But there's **one area that I always forget about**... have you ever noticed sometimes when you download something there's a '(1)' after it... (Or sometimes 2, 3, 4...) – that generally means you've **already downloaded it before**... so you guessed it... if you just **hit CTRL + J** and open up **your last downloads** you should be able to **find it in there** without having to re-download it all over again...

Top Tip

When you're struggling to find that file you downloaded last week, rather than trawl through e-mails or try to remember the web page you found it, just go to your downloads folder and check the history.

For Chrome, IE, Firefox on Windows use CTRL + J
For Safari on Mac use COMMAND + OPTION + L

It's not just you, I get quite wound up about too. Something worked perfectly well last week, and then you come in on a Monday morning and it's broken... why does that happen? Are there some magic evil elves in overnight that run round and break stuff?

Well kind of yes and no... obviously there are no **evil magic elves** (Have I had too much coffee this morning?) but usually, most nights some kind of update will have been released... occasionally these updates can break something...

I remember a time when it was a choice whether you upgraded or not... you'd get an update maybe once a year. Not the case anymore, with the internet updates can be pushed out as often as you need... I've got some software that updates every time it runs... but most stuff these days you'll find is updated once or twice a month...

You see it used to be the case that once a year you'd get a nice update, you chose when to apply it and it had been thoroughly tested before you received it. If there was a problem before the annual update was ready you'd just have to wait, or find a work around... the trouble these days is you just can't wait that long... it's big business finding security holes and vulnerabilities in software you've got to get that hole fixed ASAP.

The trouble with this is lot of stuff doesn't seem to get tested as well as maybe it did... you could argue that's because of time constraints... or because it's so easy to roll out new updates what's the point in spending a huge amount of time and resources testing something to the nth degree? – I'm sure there are many opinions on that and I don't want to open up a whole can of worms ;)

So what does this mean for you as a user? Well generally I'd recommend you keep updated, it depends on the software and how 'critical' it is to your business, for some updates we'll just run them straight in to you live environment, for others we'll run them in a **test environment**, make sure **you can still do business** as you need to, then roll them out to your **live environment**... deciding which is the best option in each case is one of the 'behind the scenes' benefits of using **a good I.T. support company**...

The good news is because it's easy and quick to release updates, if there are problems, they usually just release a new one to fix the problems caused in the previous one...

Then you get the updates which just happen, and you've not really got much control over it... you pretty much have to do them... a lot of standard software is like this – Windows Updates, Adobe Reader, Google Chrome, Office etc.... Your trouble comes when you're updating some programs and not others... that's when you start to get incompatibilities and stuff starts breaking... you think "Well I've not changed anything" and frustration sets in...

I get the sense I've prattled on a bit today, so I'll leave it there, but feel free to ask me more if you're interested...

Top Tip

Keep up to date...

The pace of change is rapid these days... the more widely used a piece of software, the more likely someone is to be looking for a way to hack it...

The bad guys out there are constantly looking for security holes in software, and software companies are constantly fixing those holes...

that's why you tend to see so many more updates these days...
You really should be keeping up to date...

Giveaway #11 – Half Price MOT

As a thank you for reading this far in to my book have a half price Computer MOT on me! Oh and if you're within the first 20, I'll pay the other half for you!

http://chrisbluntbooks.co.uk/wsh2

From: Chris Blunt chrisblunt@busstopgroup.co.uk

Sent: 1st December

Subject: **Want to know more?**

If you've found this book, and the tips in it useful, and you'd like to know more then you can sign up to my weekly top tips right here: http://chrisbluntbooks/toptips/

If you want to get in touch with me, you can reach out to me via the following ways:

Blog:

http://letsbebluntaboutit.co.uk

Website:

http://brokenstones.co.uk

http://chrisbluntbooks.co.uk

http://busstopgroup.co.uk

Twitter:

@brokestones

@ChrisAndDonald

Facebook:

http://facebook.com/brokenstonesIT

LinkedIn:

http://uk.linkedin.com/in/chrisblunt/

BrokenStones Helpdesk: (For all IT Support Enquiries)

01543 241 016

Amazon: Did you enjoy this book? If so please think about leaving me a favourable review on Amazon.

From: Chris Blunt chrisblunt@busstopgroup.co.uk

Sent: 2nd December

Subject: **An Intriguing Offer**

I've got some sad news for you... that was the last Top I.T. tip of this book...

The good news is the next one is well underway, and I'd love to feature you in it...

You've read all my book, you've seen the kind of questions people send me and the kinds of topics I cover... so why not send me your own question you'd like answered

Win a Signed Copy of my Next Book

I'm well underway with the next 52 e-mails and I'd love to feature you in the next book, all you need to do is wiz me over any kind of I.T question you'd like to be addressed and if I think it is suitable enough it may feature for the basis of one of my emails and I'll send you a signed copy of my next book with my compliments.

If there is no questions you want answered just drop me a comment on what you think of the book and as you'll have seen by the back cover there is a chance you'll get featured on here and get a copy that way.

You can ask questions or leave me feedback by visiting the following link:

http://chrisbluntbooks.co.uk/wsh2

From: Jordan Smith Jordan.smith@brokenstones.net

Sent: 04th December
Subject: **A few words from me**

I'm Jordan, I'm the new marketing apprentice for brokenStones and I'd like to thank you for picking up Chris's book. I hope it has been very useful and filled in some of the gaps of your I.T knowledge.

My first task as an apprentice was to help Chris finish his second book and get it published. It has been good fun and a great learning experience for me as I hope it has been a great read for you too. I've proof read it, helped design the front and back cover, also came up with the title (So if you notice any mistakes it's not Chris's fault ;)).

I'd like you to pass on the knowledge you've gained from this book to others, as I have.

When shI.T happens to you just keep this book by your side and you'll be back on track in no time.

Thanks for reading.

Jord.

From: Chris Blunt chrisblunt@busstopgroup.co.uk

Sent: 12th December

Subject: **The Giveaways**

Throughout this book you'll have seen the 'Giveaway' boxes, I've listed them all here in brief for your convenience. In addition if you want the whole list emailed through to you just go to **http://chrisbluntbooks.co.uk/wsh2** and I'll send you a quick and easy reference to them all...

1. **EverNote**
2. **Free Domain Check**
3. **Free Warranty Check Service**
4. **Professional Email Signature**
5. **Ask A Question**
6. **Free Password Guide**
7. **Drop Box Free Trial**
8. **Email Address Check**
9. **Free Backup Service**
10. **Help Desk Packages**
11. **Half Price MOT**

Top Tip

One Final Top Tip from me.

Please, Please, Please... if you find even just one page in this book useful...
RIP IT OUT!! Stick it on your wall... and use it...

Books are made to be used... not to sit on a shelf and get dusty...

Legal Disclaimer: I accept no liability or responsibility if you are foolish enough to try and rip a page out of your Kindle and stick that on the wall. Some Common Sense is required on your part before heeding this, or any of my advice!